More Praise for *The Truth about Lies in the Workplace*

"We live in a world of confusion and deception. *The Truth about Lies in the Workplace* will make us all successful detectives and fact checkers in our work lives. This book gave me insights int~ finding the truth and safeguarding my reputation."
—**Lee Hornick, President, Business ^   nd Program Director, The C(**

"*The Truth about Lies in th*   ing liars at work. It's about rec.   ~ work-place deception, understanc   ~~es affect the way we interpret and relate to lies   ~, and finding ways to minimize the destructive impact of lies and hidden biases. Carol Kinsey Goman brings these concepts together in ways easy to understand. Our challenge is to use this understanding to do the hard work required to create open, honest, and productive workplaces."
—**Marci Rubin, Executive Director, California Minority Counsel Program**

"Carol Kinsey Goman exposes the mechanics of deception in this powerful new handbook for workplace health and productivity. Add a live keynote or seminar with Carol, and a new era of leadership and exemplary workplace culture is within your grasp."
—**Karen Tucker, CEO, Churchill Club**

"What a fabulous topic for today's leaders. As we move toward heterarchical organizational design, there's never been a more important time to deal with deception in the workplace."
—**Watts Wacker, futurist and bestselling coauthor of *The 500 Year Delta***

"In today's hyperconnected world, transparency and trust in the workplace are critical. Carol Kinsey Goman clearly understands the power of honest, collaborative leadership. And that's no lie."
—**Linda Kaplan Thaler, Chairman, and Robin Koval, CEO, Publicis Kaplan Thaler**

"Carol Kinsey Goman offers a thoughtful, often counterintuitive, and actionable analysis of lying in the workplace and in life. She is an exceptionally good business writer. Her work is practical and useful. I highly recommend Goman's *The Truth about Lies in the Workplace* to anyone who manages people."
—**Timothy Askew, CEO, Corporate Rain International**

"In this groundbreaking work, Carol Kinsey Goman, PhD, boldly enters a topic that has been taboo for far too long and reveals the tools and tactics necessary to spot the liar in our midst. We attempt to hire warriors only to realize too late that we have hired a cunning liar. Now there is no excuse! *The Truth about Lies in the Workplace* is a game changer and a long-overdue weapon in the tool kit of every HR professional."

—**Brad Szollose, award-winning author of** *Liquid Leadership*

"People lie for different reasons. It can be driven by fear, greed, or even an organizational culture that encourages it. No matter what the reason, lying destroys employee morale and ultimately the bottom line. *The Truth about Lies in the Workplace* gives you the tools to cut through to the truth and helps you determine what to do when you spot lies."

—**Jon Peters, President, The Institute for Management Studies, and CEO, AthenaOnline**

"Goman's great book is far more than a primer on how to recalibrate your BS detector. It will completely reframe what you know about lying while providing powerful perspectives and practices on how to nurture trust in the workplace. I promise you'll be surprised and enlightened."

—**Chip R. Bell, coauthor of** *Wired and Dangerous*

The Truth
about Lies in the
Workplace

Other books by Carol Kinsey Goman

■ *This Isn't the Company I Joined:*
How to Lead in an Organization Turned Upside Down

■ *The Nonverbal Advantage:*
Secrets and Science of Body Language at Work

■ *The Silent Language of Leaders:*
How Body Language Can Help—or Hurt—How You Lead

The **Truth** about **Lies** in the **Workplace**

How to Spot Liars and What to Do about Them

Carol Kinsey Goman

BK

Berrett–Koehler Publishers, Inc.
San Francisco
a BK Life book

Berrett-Koehler Publishers, Inc.
235 Montgomery Street, Suite 650, San Francisco, CA 94104-2916
Tel: (415) 288-0260   Fax: (415) 362-2512   www.bkconnection.com

Ordering Information

Quantity sales. Special discounts are available on quantity purchases by corporations, associations, and others. For details, contact the "Special Sales Department" at the Berrett-Koehler address above.

Individual sales. Berrett-Koehler publications are available through most bookstores. They can also be ordered directly from Berrett-Koehler: Tel: (800) 929-2929; Fax: (802) 864-7626; www.bkconnection.com.

Orders for college textbook/course adoption use. Please contact Berrett-Koehler: Tel: (800) 929-2929; Fax: (802) 864-7626.

Orders by U.S. trade bookstores and wholesalers. Please contact Ingram Publisher Services, Tel: (800) 509-4887; Fax: (800) 838-1149; E-mail: customer.service@ingrampublisherservices.com; or visit www.ingrampublisherservices.com/Ordering for details about electronic ordering.

Berrett-Koehler and the BK logo are registered trademarks of Berrett-Koehler Publishers, Inc.

Printed in the United States of America

Berrett-Koehler books are printed on long-lasting acid-free paper. When it is available, we choose paper that has been manufactured by environmentally responsible processes. These may include using trees grown in sustainable forests, incorporating recycled paper, minimizing chlorine in bleaching, or recycling the energy produced at the paper mill.

Library of Congress Cataloging-in-Publication Data
Goman, Carol Kinsey.
    The truth about lies in the workplace : how to spot liars and what to do about them / Carol Kinsey Goman.
        pages cm
    Includes bibliographical references and index.
    ISBN 978-1-60994-837-5 (pbk.)
    1. Communication in organizations. 2. Deception. 3. Truthfulness and falsehood.
    4. Body language. 5. Interpersonal communication. 6. Psychology, Industrial. I. Title.
    HD30.3.G645 2013
    650.1'3—dc23
                                                    2013004889

18   17   16   15   14   13   10   9   8   7   6   5   4   3   2   1

Cover design by Karen Marquardt. Cover image by Focus Stock Fotografico/Getty Images. Interior illustrations by James P. Welch. Interior design and composition by Gary Palmatier, Ideas to Images. Elizabeth von Radics, copyeditor; Mike Mollett, proofreader; Alexandra Nickerson, indexer.

To Skip, always and forever

*And to Toni Franklin, Ellen Vaughan,
and Joyce Turley Nicholas—
my incredibly special cheerleaders*

Contents

Introduction

For the past two years I have been a contributor to Forbes.com. I write articles about body language—its impact on a leader's effectiveness in managing change, engaging employees, leading collaboration, negotiating, and communicating with a multicultural workforce. My more popular entries usually receive 10,000 to 20,000 hits.

On April 11, 2012, I posted the blog "12 Ways to Spot a Liar at Work." Within 10 days the post had been viewed 262,929 times. Clearly, the number of hits showed that this topic struck a chord with my business and leadership audiences.

It also reflected my growing interest in the subject. I had been trained as a therapist and knew how to track, mirror, and analyze nonverbal cues. In my private practice and later as a leadership coach, I became adept at spotting contradiction—noting those places where a client's words and body language were out of sync. I became a fan of Paul Ekman, the foremost authority in emotions research, nonverbal communication, and the role of microexpressions in lie detection; and most recently Patryk Wezowski, founder of the Center for Body Language in Antwerp, and his program for detecting microexpressions in workplace settings. I followed a variety of other researchers as they reported on the lying behaviors of children, profiled the (sometimes surprising) qualities of convincing liars, and used functional magnetic resonance imaging (fMRI) machines to track what happens in a person's brain when telling a lie. In addition, my 25 years as a lecturer in more than 100 companies in 24 countries provided me with real-world knowledge about the impact of deception in the workplace.

I assumed that, given what I already knew, writing a book on this topic would be easy.

I was wrong.

The deeper I delved into the most recent studies on deception from neuroscientists, social psychologists, and university researchers, the more I discovered how little I really knew. I began by thinking that lying in the workplace was an aberration that could be eliminated; instead I found that lying was created by evolution and driven by social necessity—and that we couldn't operate in a business environment (or any other environment) without some forms of it. I thought that I could divide the workplace into categories—the deceitful "them" and the truthful "us"—but found that there is no such clear-cut distinction. I believed that I was honest with myself, only to discover that no one is. I felt I was a perceptive and objective observer, but I discovered that like everyone else I hold unconscious biases that are pervasive and powerful enough to distort reality.

When I sent out a "deception in the workplace" questionnaire, I received 547 responses that added to my growing knowledge—this time from firsthand accounts—about the negative effects that destructive lies have on individuals, teams, and organizations. I learned that many people work (happily and productively) in organizations with ethical leadership and trustworthy co-workers. But I also learned that a majority does not: 67 percent of respondents said that they have lost confidence in the truthfulness of their senior leaders, 53 percent admitted that they don't trust their managers, and 51 percent believed that their co-workers regularly lied.

The Truth about Lies in the Workplace describes what I have discovered so far about this nuanced and fascinating topic. The following is a brief overview.

Chapter 1, "Liars at Work," lays a framework for the book by giving an overview of the (positive and negative) nature, pervasiveness, and consequences of lies at work. Chapter 2, "Deception Detection: 50 Ways to Spot a Liar," teaches you the signs of increased stress and anxiety that most often accompany deception and explains the verbal and nonverbal cues that are most likely to indicate a falsehood. Chapter 3, "Why We Believe Liars and Play into Their Hands," explains how our vanities, assumptions, prejudices, rationalizations, and self-deceptions set us up to be duped. Chapter 4, "How to Deal With Liars," gives practical advice and options for responding when someone lies to or about you. Chapter 5, "Do You Look Like a Liar?," offers body language tips to help you project your true competence and confidence—and to ensure that feeling anxious, introverted, or shy doesn't inadvertently signal untrustworthiness. Chapter 6, "Reducing Lies in the Workplace," includes examples of how leaders at all levels of the organization are reducing destructive lies and encouraging candor.

I think you'll find this book a real eye-opener. I did, researching it. I'd love to hear about your experience with lies and deception (or with honesty and trust) in your workplace. Please contact me at cgoman@ckg.com with comments and questions.

CHAPTER 1

Liars at Work

YOU WORK WITH A BUNCH OF LIARS.

You're a liar, yourself.

So am I.

That's the truth.

But wouldn't it be nice if it weren't? Wouldn't it be convenient if the workforce were divided neatly into "us" versus "them"? We, of course, would be the good guys who were always up front and truthful. They would be the rotten apples whose destructive lies betray the confidence placed in them and ruin everything for the rest of us. If that scenario were valid, imagine how simple it would be to create totally candid corporate cultures: the human resources (HR) department could develop a test for truthfulness to eliminate liars before they were hired, promotions could be awarded to the most honest employees, and alert managers could weed out any extrawily deceivers who somehow slipped in and were later exposed.

But if the truth is that we're *all* liars—if the line between "us" and "them" is not as definitive as we'd like to think—how in the world do we deal with lies in the workplace? That's the question that makes this subject so provocative and leads to a host of issues that I will be addressing throughout the book.

There is no universally agreed upon definition of *lie, lying, deception,* or *liar,* and each of us has his or her own opinion about what constitutes a small, inoffensive fib; a diplomatic white lie; or a big, damaging slander. In this book I use the words *deception* and *lie* interchangeably; however, I view *deception* as the broader umbrella term that includes every imaginable way to mislead, whereas *lying* refers to specific acts of generating falsehoods or omissions for the purpose of deception. With this as a starting point, my goal is not only to help you spot liars in the workplace but also to help you determine which lies and liars can be overlooked or forgiven and which are truly destructive and need to be dealt with seriously.

Development of a Liar

In *Why We Lie: The Evolutionary Roots of Deception and the Unconscious Mind,* David Livingstone Smith poses the theory that lying is deeply embedded in our subconscious as a result of evolution.[1] In evolutionary terms, being a successful liar constitutes a "selective advantage"—which means simply that our ancestors who didn't develop the knack for deception died off and those who survived by lying passed on stronger and stronger genes for this ability.

But being born with a predisposition for deception doesn't mean we are born knowing *how* to lie. The fact is, we have to learn that skill. New research shows that lying may even be a positive developmental milestone. A Canadian study of 1,200 children ages two to 17 suggests that those who are able to lie successfully have reached an important developmental stage because only children who have advanced cognitive development are able to carry out the complex juggling act that involves saying one thing while keeping the truth in the back of their minds. Only one-fifth of the two-year-olds tested in the study were able to do that, whereas at age four 90 percent were capable of lying advantageously. The rate increased with age to a peak at 12. By the time children are teenagers, they become even more adept at lying—moving from basic deceptions to quite intricate fabrications.[2]

When we finally grow up, do we at last see the error of our youthful ways and take the honesty pledge? Of course not! This is a life skill we're talking about. We go right on lying—either occasionally, frequently, habitually, or pathologically—for the rest of our lives.

Most of the lies we tell are self-serving, meaning they are lies that benefit us: the job candidate who exaggerates his or her accomplishments does so to look more qualified for the position. Some are intended to benefit others: the co-worker who compliments a nervous colleague does so to put him or her at ease. And some lies are a mixture: the manager who tells competing candidates that he backs each of them is wanting to boost the self-esteem of both people, but he also wants to be "on the winning side" regardless of which candidate gets the job.

In the workplace people fib, flatter, fabricate, prevaricate, and equivocate. They take liberties with, embellish, bend, and stretch the truth. They boast, conceal, falsify, omit, spread gossip, misinform, or cover up embarrassing (perhaps even unethical) acts. They lie to avoid accepting responsibility, to build status and power, to "protect" others from hearing a negative truth, to preserve a sense of autonomy, to keep their jobs, to get out of unwanted work, to get on the good side of the boss, or to be perceived as "team players" when their main motivation is self-interest. They lie because they're under pressure to perform and because, as one co-worker observed about his teammates, "they lack the guts to tell the boss that what is being asked isn't doable."

Some types of people are better than others at lying. If you are creative, you are one of them—not because creativity makes you more likely to be dishonest but because you're probably good at convincing yourself of your own lies. If you have a charismatic or dominant personality (as many C-suite executives do), you probably also have a special capacity to deceive—which doesn't mean you lie more than others; it just suggests that when you do, you are more skilled at it.

If you're an extrovert, you lie at a higher rate than do introverts. If you are intelligent, you can think strategically and plan ahead like a good chess player—and you can better handle the cognitive load imposed by lying. If you are manipulative or overly concerned about the impression you are making on others, you tell more lies. If you are adept at reading body language, you are also adept at sensing when other people are getting suspicious. And if you have a good memory, you are less likely to be tripped up by your falsehoods.

You may even be in a profession that produces "polished" liars. If you are an actor, poker player, evangelist, salesperson, politician, marketer, negotiator, coach, company spokesperson, lawyer, or (my profession) a professional speaker, you have probably learned to "bluff" convincingly.

Four Types of Liars

Occasional liars. Most of us fall into this category. We don't like to lie but do it every now and then. Occasional liars feel the most uncomfortable about lying and are the easiest to detect through the verbal and nonverbal cues that I detail in chapter 2.

Frequent liars. These are more comfortable with lying, even though they know it's wrong. Because they are more practiced, their lies are more difficult to detect.

Habitual liars. They tell lies automatically and effortlessly. Their deception comes across as "natural" behavior because for these people it is. But often they get lazy or sloppy with their content, and that is what trips them up.

Pathological liars. This is the hardest group to detect because they lie compulsively—often for no apparent advantage—and have totally bought into the veracity of their own lies. Fortunately, this kind of liar is rare and far less likely to be encountered in the course of normal business dealings.

Workplace Lies at All Levels of the Organization

Workplace lies run the gamut, from everyday fibs to whoppers, and from benign to destructive. Small lies are easily forgiven or overlooked: "My manager gave out an earlier due date for the completion of a project than was necessary. She knew that some people would procrastinate, and she wanted to make sure the work was done on schedule." Big lies destroy trust and are almost never forgotten or forgiven: "My boss assured me that my position was secure—then he accidentally copied me on an e-mail about interviewing my replacement."

One thing to keep in mind is that not all untruths are lies. Different people recall different details from the same event. That's why eyewitness statements are often contradictory, and why two co-workers can attend the same business conference and come back with two very different opinions of the event.

Liars deliberately choose to mislead others, and lies may be encountered throughout a person's career, from résumé inaccuracies when applying for a job to disingenuous answers on exit interviews when leaving an organization. And they can occur at any level of the organization. From my survey of 547 business professionals, the following are the most common workplace lies. (All of the quotes in this section are from anonymous survey respondents.)

Lies from Senior Leaders

Leaders' lies matter most because the behavior of leaders has a greater impact on more people and because others model that behavior. Of the respondents to my survey, 67 percent said that the senior leaders of their organizations didn't always tell the truth. Leadership lies cited most often were those of omission and misrepresentation—executives either didn't tell the whole truth or they presented an overly optimistic view of the company's current state and future prospects.

Withholding crucial information. The number one complaint from employees is that executives lie by telling half-truths and omitting negative information, especially during a merger or restructuring or at any time the organization is facing potential layoffs.

"I work with the senior leadership team on a daily basis, so I'm pretty much in the communication loop. I've seen members lie blatantly to their own staff members about layoffs and plant closures that have actually been decided on weeks before and in some cases have already become hot rumors on the company grapevine. Why bother lying about something people know is going to happen? Company culture, I guess. 'It's what we've always done.' Why? You tell me!"

"Our leaders don't provide the whole truth about anticipated impacts of organizational changes. In fact, the information they do present is so garbled and wrapped up in big words, it's like listening to politicians trying to put something over on us."

Glossing over the truth. Whether you call it "corporate spin," "excessive optimism," or "irrational exuberance," talking about things going well when they obviously aren't is the second most frequently observed deceptive behavior of corporate leaders.

"Board reports are always routinely revised to present a better picture of the company's status and performance. It's expected. I know because I was part of the senior leadership team charged with overseeing the rewrites."

"The executives keep saying that things are fine and there will be other work to do. Meanwhile they keep outsourcing our jobs. Do they think we don't notice?"

Lies from Managers

The relationship between manager and staff is the most crucial for employee satisfaction and engagement. As is often noted, people rarely quit their jobs due to disputes with organizational policies; they quit because they work for ineffective or uncaring bosses. In my deception survey, 53 percent of respondents said that their immediate supervisor lies to them. The most common lies were avoiding responsibility for mistakes or failures and, conversely, taking too much credit for team successes. Managers were also accused of not keeping promises and of lying because they were afraid to admit that they were fallible.

Avoiding responsibility. "My boss said it was my fault, but she was the one who missed the deadline—not me."

"He blames others to cover himself in front of his own boss."

Taking undue credit. "My manager takes credit for the efforts of the entire team. One day I'd like to see how he gets on without us."

"We do all the work. She takes all the bows."

Not keeping promises. "My boss said she'd write a letter of recommendation. I reminded her several times, but she never followed through."

"I was promised that I could go to the training seminar, but when the time came my boss made some lame excuse."

Not admitting fallibility. "My boss routinely lies to the executive team because she wants them to think she can handle everything. In reality she is too weak to tell them what they don't want to hear."

"He just makes things up. I think he's afraid of looking uninformed by admitting he doesn't know."

Lies from Colleagues

Because we interact with them so closely during the workday, almost without realizing it we subject our immediate colleagues to more or less continual judgment regarding their performances and behaviors. Most of the time, we find that co-worker lies are small, insignificant, and easily forgiven or forgotten, involving nothing more serious than excuses for missed deadlines or failure to follow through on requests. But over time a pattern of these seemingly inconsequential lies can erode workplace relationships and inhibit teamwork.

About half (51 percent) of survey respondents said that they have had to deal with colleagues who lied to and about them on a variety of matters a good deal more serious than missed deadlines. Especially egregious to my participants were backstabbing behaviors, lies to hide unethical acts, and deliberately withholding or misreporting information.

Backstabbing. "The other department head thanked me for my idea, then told our boss that I'd stolen it from her. Luckily, I had documents that proved otherwise."

"My co-worker made up terrible things about another person and said that I started the rumor."

Unethical behavior. "One of my colleagues lies consistently on his expense reports, pads them, and uses extra days of travel to get frequent-flyer miles so that he can take his wife on vacations."

"She inflates her expense account excessively for food and drinks—but when I asked her about it, she said that there was an 'unwritten rule' that this was okay so long as she didn't exceed her budget."

Information hoarding and misinformation. "Some people on the team hoard information or misinform other team members as a way of making themselves feel more powerful and in control."

"I wasn't invited to the meeting—deliberately, I'm pretty sure—so of course I couldn't come up with the details when my manager asked for them later. I felt like an idiot. I also felt like someone on that team has it in for me."

What about You?

According to a 1997 study jointly sponsored by the American Society of Chartered Life Underwriters (now the Society of Financial Services Professionals) and the Ethics and Compliance Officer Association, 48 percent of the workers interviewed admitted that they had engaged in one or more unethical or illegal actions during the year—including lying to a supervisor or direct report, deceiving customers, covering up incidents, taking credit for co-workers' ideas, and faking sick days.[3]

When I talk with managers about the worst kind of lies they hear from their staffs, they often mention lies of omission: "There is nothing worse than getting blindsided by a project that has gone off course."

What about you? Do you always tell the truth? When I put that question to my survey participants, 53 percent admitted lying—primarily to cover up job performance inadequacies, to control time, or as part of a job or career strategy.

Lying to cover up job performance. "I lied and said that I was almost finished with the project when I hadn't even started."

"I didn't want to look unprepared, so I said I knew all about the situation. But I knew nothing."

Lying to control time. "When I'm at a meeting and find I am wasting my time, I leave, saying I have to attend another meeting. I also lie about my agenda when I don't want to attend meetings. Or sometimes I will pretend to forget a meeting. I use this technique only for meetings that I view as a waste of my time, however. I do attend important meetings."

"I'll say I'm sick when what I really need is a sanity break."

Lying as part of job or career strategy. "I assure my staff that everything is fine, even when I know it isn't. It is my role in the organization to play dumb about big executive decisions until I've been told when the announcement is scheduled; I then tell whatever lies I have to to keep panic from spreading."

"I flatter people to make them feel more important so they'll be more likely to pay attention to me and listen to what I have to say."

"I said I resigned 'for professional growth reasons.' It would have been career suicide to tell the truth."

Liars, Lies, and Diversity

Although there hasn't been a lot of research to determine if gender, socioeconomic class, or race or culture changes the frequency or the type of lie being told, here are a few preliminary findings.

Gender

Who are the biggest liars—men or women? I've uncovered no valid research to suggest that men and women lie at different rates—with the exception of one study on deception in an economic setting: researchers at the Stockholm School of Economics found that men are significantly more likely than women to lie to secure a monetary benefit.[4] There is, however, wider agreement that men and women lie differently.

Men tell more self-centered lies. They lie about their accomplishments, salaries, and status in an attempt to appear more powerful or interesting than they are.

Women also tell self-centered lies, but—and this is most apparent in their dealings with other women—they tell more "other-oriented" lies and are more likely to fake positive feelings. In my deception survey, women frequently reported lying to protect someone's feelings: "It's something I'm working on. I know how important it is to be totally candid with my staff—especially during their performance reviews—but I still hate to say anything that makes someone feel bad."

Socioeconomic Class

A series of studies conducted by psychologists at the University of California, Berkeley and the University of Toronto in Canada found that people who considered themselves upper class (as determined by a standardized questionnaire) were more likely than lower-class participants to make unethical choices, such as cheating to increase their chances of winning a prize.[5]

They were also more likely to lie (by omission) during a job interview. In this role-playing study, participants were assigned the role of an employer negotiating a salary with a job candidate seeking long-term employment. Among other things, they were told that the job would soon be eliminated and that they were free to convey that information to the candidate. Upper-class participants were more likely to deceive job candidates by withholding this information.

The only factor found to supersede class in determining unethical behavior was the subject's attitude about greed. When participants were primed to think about the advantages of greed and were then presented with bad-behavior-in-the-workplace scenarios—such as stealing cash, accepting bribes, and overcharging customers—participants from lower classes were just as likely to engage in unethical behavior as the upper-class cohort.

Lies across Cultures

The word *culture* refers primarily to a set of shared social values and assumptions that determine acceptable or "normal" behavior within a defined society, such as a nation, commonwealth, tribe, or religious community. These values also serve a given society as a benchmark by which to judge the behavior of others.

All cultures can be situated in relation to one another through the styles in which they communicate. *Low-context cultures* (German, Scandinavian, American, English, and Canadian) communicate predominately through verbal statements and the written word. Low-context communication is explicit, direct, and precise, with little reliance on the unstated or implied. In *high-context cultures* (Japanese, Chinese, Arab, Greek, and Mexican), communication depends more on sensitivity to nonverbal behaviors—body language, proximity, and the use of pauses and silence—and on environmental cues, such as the relationship of the participants, what has occurred in the past, who is in attendance, and the time and place of the communication. So when a high-context culture thinks that an understanding has been reached because of who participated in the meeting, low-context-culture participants may be waiting for a formal agreement to be signed.

In international business dealings, I've also noticed that the way different cultures handle accountability and responsibility can make it seem as if someone is lying even when they are not. For example, in the Japanese culture, responding yes to a question often means "I heard you" and *not* "I agree with you." I've seen this type of misunderstanding lead Western team members to think that their Japanese counterparts have lied to them or are not honoring their word.

Some nonverbal signals are unique to a particular culture and can bring confusion to international dealings. Emblematic gestures fall into this category. For example, what we in the United States think of as a positive gesture—the "okay" sign with thumb and forefinger together creating a circle—has very different meanings in other cultures. In France it means "worthless" or "zero," in Japan it stands for money, and in other countries it is lewd or obscene. Other signals—such as the amount of eye contact deemed proper, head nods (to signal *yes*), the accepted physical space between conversation partners, the amount of touch allowed, and the level of emotional display—that feel so right in one culture can be viewed as inappropriate or even deceptive in another.

The very definitions of honesty and deception can cause significant conflicts in intercultural relationships. A study by four universities (two in Canada and two in China) examined cross-cultural differences in Canadian and Chinese concepts of lying about certain behaviors.[6] The biggest difference the researchers found was in the area of untruthful statements made to conceal one's own good deeds. Nearly all Canadians labeled these as lies, but many Chinese allowed untruthful statements made for modesty's sake to fall outside the realm of lying. Another noteworthy finding was that the Canadians gave significantly more positive ratings to confessing misdeeds than did the Chinese. Most of the Canadians highly valued admitting mistakes and taking responsibility for them. Most of the Chinese believed that while confession was commendable it did not negate the bad behavior of lying.

Another joint study, this one by Michigan State University and the University of California, Santa Barbara, investigated the relationship between American and Korean cultures in their evaluation of truth and deception.[7] One finding reflected the communication differences in high-context and low-context cultures. Koreans converse less directly and clearly, relying on other factors like personal bonds, previous dealings, and nonverbal cues to add significance. Because Koreans were more accustomed to producing and comprehending indirect meaning, they tended to judge ambiguous messages as less deceptive than low-context Americans who expected truthful statements to be specific and complete.

Consequences of Lying

Despite the fact that the workplace is awash in deception, I don't mean to suggest that we should give a free pass to lies that do real harm. As discussed, some lies actually preserve the social order and can even be selfless. From this point on, however, we focus on those lies that seriously damage relationships and organizations. I realize that this distinction can be like the "I know it when I see it" test for rudeness, but most human beings are extremely nuanced in gauging another's selfishness as a liar. The boss who gives you a false deadline because she knows you procrastinate might actually seem canny and clever to you. The boss who gives you an early deadline so that she can take credit for your work is much harder to forgive. The early deadline might be the same in each example, but only one is hurtful and harmful. Unless I say differently from this point on, you can assume that I mean "painfully selfish, destructive lie" when I use the simple word *lie*. Life is too short to worry too much about the other kind!

With this in mind, I hate lying. I don't mean I hate the "I'd *love* to be interviewed on your 3 a.m. radio show" or the "It's *no trouble* to create a custom-tailored program outline so that you can decide if you want to hire me as a speaker" kind of lie. I'm perfectly comfortable with those. But I hate lies that force me to remember conflicting stories and that I fear will shame or embarrass me if found out. Those lies are too stressful and take too much of my emotional, physical, and mental energy.

I also hate what lies can do to others—to the individuals who tell them, to those who are duped by them, and to teams, departments, and organizations that deal with the repercussions. The following are a few consequences to consider.

Lies are bad for your health. Psychologists at the University of Notre Dame conducted an "honesty experiment" in which 110 individuals, ages 18 to 71, participated over a 10-week period.[8] Each week they came to a laboratory to complete a health assessment and take a lie detector test. When researchers tallied the number of physical and mental health complaints, the study found that as people increased the number of lies they told, their health declined. Conversely, when lies went down, the subjects' health improved.

Deceiving others increases self-deception. Researchers at Harvard Business School found that those who cheat on tests are more likely than non-cheaters to rationalize their superior performance into a genuine sign of intelligence.[9] This unconscious act of self-deception, while providing a short-term psychological boost, comes with a longer-term price to pay; when asked to predict their own future performances, the cheaters erroneously presumed that they would perform as well as they had previously—and of course couldn't.

Lies can destroy your reputation. In the era of personal branding, two things are most important to success: your professional network and your reputation. Nothing can weaken a network or destroy a reputation faster than being exposed as a liar.

Lies can destroy your career. Embellishing your résumé or company track record may not seem like such a big deal, until you realize how many people who rose by this method also came crashing down. RadioShack's chief executive officer (CEO), David Edmondson, lost his job in 2006 after acknowledging that he lied about academic degrees listed on the company's website.[10] Notre Dame football coach George O'Leary resigned after five days on the job when it came to light that he had falsified academic and athletic credentials.[11]

Then there's the more recent case of Yahoo's CEO Scott Thompson, who was asked to leave the company after a fake degree on his résumé was discovered.[12] Whether Thompson embellished his bio with a college major he didn't earn (his actual accounting degree was changed to include one in computer science) or signed his name to a document someone else falsified, the lie cost him a flourishing career. Thompson had claimed the false credential when he was president of PayPal. After he joined Yahoo, his official bio containing the double major became part of the company's annual report filed to the Securities and Exchange Commission, a document that CEOs must personally attest is truthful.

The recipient of a lie feels betrayed. In many cases, a lie is a violation of trust in a trust-dependent relationship. Bernard Madoff operated a Ponzi scheme that defrauded thousands of investors out of billions of dollars. His victims' justifiable anger was tinged with feelings of deep betrayal. They lost hard-earned money that they thought they'd placed in safe hands because they believed Madoff's lies.

But you don't have to lose your life savings to feel betrayed by a liar. Whenever your trust in someone is destroyed by his or her lies, there is almost always an element of betrayal. This is also why it is so difficult to ever trust that person again.

Lies of omission hinder collaboration. Collaboration depends on knowledge sharing. When team leaders or colleagues withhold information, it affects each individual's ability to do his or her part and to contribute to the goals of the team. Omission is especially damaging to collaborative efforts when some (the chosen few) are given information and others are excluded.

Lies weaken productivity and profits. Inside organizational cultures that encourage lies and deception, or at least don't actively discourage them, something insidious begins to happen: previously dedicated workers become less committed to company goals; skepticism builds (I've watched an audience play "buzzword bingo" while listening to executives' speeches); employees increasingly complain to one another; absenteeism increases; productivity, innovation, and customer service plummet; and, eventually, so do profits.

Lies are expensive. According to the Association of Certified Fraud Examiners, a typical organization loses 5 percent of its revenue to fraud—a potential global fraud loss of $3.5 trillion.[13]

Lies can threaten an entire industry. A 2012 *New York Times* article, "As Libor Fault-Finding Grows, It Is Now Every Bank for Itself," states: "Major banks, which often band together when facing government scrutiny, are now turning on one another as an international investigation into the manipulation of [interbank borrowing] interest rates gains momentum. With billions of dollars and their reputations on the line, financial institutions have been spreading the blame in recent meetings with authorities, according to government and bank officials with knowledge of the matter."[14]

So, you work with a bunch of liars. You indulge in a bit of lying yourself. Most of that lying—yours, mine, and everyone else's—is either benign or falls under the heading of the pettiest of petty crime. But not all of it. Remember Nick Leeson, the former derivatives broker whose fraudulent and unauthorized speculative trading caused the collapse of Barings? Remember Lehman Brothers, whose bankruptcy triggered a chain reaction that produced the worst financial crisis and economic downturn in 70 years? Remember Kenneth Lay, Jeffrey Skilling, and Andrew Fastow, whose use of accounting loopholes and improper financial reporting left thousands of Enron employees and investors holding the bag?

No one spotted them until it was too late. And too late is the thing we all want to avoid. By learning the verbal and nonverbal signals that most liars exhibit, you can develop your internal lie-detecting ability and increase your chances of spotting liars at work. Chapter 2 will help you do that.

CHAPTER 2

Deception Detection: 50 Ways to Spot a Liar

YOUR BOSS TELLS YOU, "THIS CHANGE IS FOR THE BEST," BUT as she speaks you notice her awkward body posture and forced smile. Is she being honest with you?

Your co-worker says he'd be happy to help you with your project, but he seems to pause a long time before answering—and while he's talking, his eyes stay focused on his computer monitor. Can you trust what he says?

"You can count on my support."

"It wasn't my fault."

"You are next in line for a promotion."

Really?

Wouldn't it be great to know when you're being lied to? And wouldn't it be nice if exposing falsehoods were as easy as it is portrayed on television shows like *The Mentalist* and *NCIS*? Of course, human beings are more complex—and subtly devious—in real life than they are as portrayed on television. As frequently encountered as deception is in the real world, its detection for most people remains as much a matter of intuition as of science.

It's Not Lie Detection—It's Stress Detection

There is no single verbal or nonverbal behavior that automatically means a person is lying. In fact, much of "lie detection" is actually "stress detection."

The mind has to work a lot harder to generate a false response. That is, to tell a lie the brain first has to stop itself from telling the truth, then create the deception, and then deal with the accompanying emotions of anxiety, guilt, and fear of being caught. So, when a person is attempting to deceive, he or she (especially if basically honest) is more likely to feel cognitively challenged—guilty, anxious, or insecure—than someone who is telling the truth. And because lying is taxing on the human brain, most of us are rather bad liars who signal our deceptions with verbal and nonverbal stress cues.

Lying and the Stress Response

For the vast majority of individuals you work with, the act of lying will trigger a heightened (and observable) stress response. But here's what complicates matters:

- Not all people demonstrate the same degree of emotion.

- Not all liars (especially if polished or pathological) display readily detectable signs of stress or guilt.

- Not all lies trigger a stress reaction. Social lies, for example, are so much a part of daily life that they hardly ever distress the sender.

We also know that truthful people can exhibit anxiety for a variety of perfectly innocent reasons, including (ironically) the fear of not being believed or discomfort speaking about embarrassing or emotionally arousing topics. For example, I'd expect both an innocent and a guilty person to exhibit signs of heightened anxiety when being questioned about a sexual harassment complaint. There is a further complication: if a person really believes that the lie being told is *not* a lie, there is no way that you (or a polygraph, for that matter) can spot that falsehood.

So, there is no guarantee that you'll be able to identify every lie you hear, but I can help you become more keenly alert both to the signs of increased stress and anxiety that most often accompany deception as well as to the verbal cues that are most likely to indicate a falsehood. As you increase your ability to spot these signals, you'll begin to automatically pinpoint and monitor behaviors that you feel need to be investigated—indications of concealed thoughts, feelings, or opinions suggesting that the whole story is not being told.

Begin with a Baseline

The first and most important step in deception detection is learning a person's *baseline* behavior under relaxed or generally stress-free conditions so that you can compare it with the expressions, gestures, and other signals that are apparent only when that person is under stress. Experienced interrogators looking to identify guilt or innocence begin by asking a series of nonthreatening questions while observing how the subject reacts when there is no reason to lie. Then, when more crucial issues get introduced, they watch for changes in behavior that may indicate deception around key points—or at least indicate areas that need to be further explored.

In a business setting, you can follow a similar path. It takes only a few minutes to get a feel for how someone acts in a relaxed or neutral setting, and the best time to do this is before the negotiation, interview, or meeting starts—for instance while having coffee and making small talk. While you are chatting informally, notice how the other person's body looks when he's relaxed. What is his normal amount of eye contact and his blink rate? What kind of gestures does he use most frequently? What posture does he assume when he's comfortable? What is his pace of speech and tone of voice?

If you ask a few questions that make the person recall factual information—"Who referred you to me?" "How many years have you been working as a consultant?" "How did you hear about this job offer?"—you can note if his or her eyes move to a preferred side when accessing truthful answers. It's only when you know someone's behavioral baseline for candor that you become adept at spotting meaningful deviations—and possible deception—later in the meeting.

Even a lie-seeking computer system relies on a baseline. Computer scientists at the University at Buffalo (State University of New York) developed lie detection software that tracks eye movements and blink rates and correctly detects deceit more than 80 percent of the time.[1] The system employs a statistical technique to model how people move their eyes in two distinct situations: during regular conversation (their baseline) and while fielding a question designed to prompt a lie. It was found that people whose pattern of eye movements changed between the first and second scenarios were often lying, whereas those who maintained consistent eye movement were most likely telling the truth.

Look for Alignment

When thoughts and words are in tune—when people believe what they are saying—you see it corroborated in their body language. Their gestures and expressions are in alignment with what is being said. You may also spot *incongruence,* where gestures *contradict* words—a side-to-side headshake while saying yes or a shoulder shrug as your boss tells you he is "fully committed to this initiative." (A shrug of one or both shoulders while making a direct statement suggests that the person doesn't believe or is not convinced of the accuracy of the facts being presented.) Often verbal/nonverbal incongruence is a sign of intentional deceit. At the very least, it shows that there's an inner conflict of some sort between what someone is thinking and what he or she is saying.

Recognize the Seven Basic Emotions

There are seven basic emotions that are shared, recognized, and expressed in the same way around the world. Discovered and categorized by Paul Ekman and his research colleagues, the universal emotional expressions are joy, surprise, sadness, anger, fear, disgust, and contempt.[2] Liars often try to fake emotional displays, but the following is what you'll see when they are genuine.

Joy. The muscles of the cheeks rise, the eyes narrow, lines appear at the corners of the eyes, and the corners of the mouth turn up.

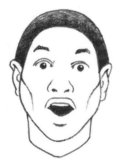

Surprise. The eyebrows rise, and there is a slight raising of the upper eyelids and a dropping of the lower jaw.

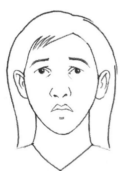

Sadness. The eyelids droop as the inner corners of the brows rise and (in extreme sorrow) draw together, and the corners of the lips pull down.

Anger. The eyebrows are pulled together and lowered, the lower eyelid is tensed, the eyes glare, and the lips tighten, appearing thinner.

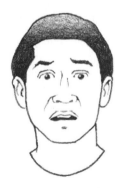

Fear. The eyebrows draw together and rise, the upper eyelid rises, the lower eyelid tenses, and the lips stretch horizontally.

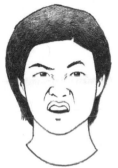

Disgust. The nose wrinkles, the upper lip rises, and the corners of the mouth turn down.

Contempt. This is the only unilateral expression. The cheek muscles on one side of the face contract, and one corner of the mouth turns up. (Contempt signals a sense of moral superiority.)

Whenever any of these emotions is strongly felt, its expression is intense and can last up to four seconds. But emotional displays in corporate settings are often subtle and fleeting, and very brief *microexpressions* (lasting only a fraction of a second) are difficult to catch if you haven't been trained to do so. But if you ever catch a fleeting expression that contradicts a verbal statement, it is a valid indicator that you'd be wise to believe what you see and not what you hear.

Emotions that are not genuinely felt often show up in expressions that don't use all of the muscles in the face that are typically employed. For example, a smile that doesn't include the eye muscles is not a felt smile. In monitoring emotional reactions, also look for simulated emotions, where people try to convince you they feel a certain way by simulating the facial expression associated with that feeling. For example, keep an eye out for the "terribly sincere furrowed brow" and for the exaggerated display of anger that feels somehow excessive, as liars tend to go in for those two. Remember too that any expression displayed for more than five to 10 seconds is almost certainly being faked.

Consider the Context

The meaning of nonverbal cues changes as the context changes. You can't begin to understand someone's behavior without considering the circumstances under which it occurs.

Imagine this scene: You are interviewing a job candidate. You ask easy questions and, in response, get relaxed body language and straightforward answers. Then you ask a complex question. The interviewee hesitates, frowns, and crosses her arms. But is she about to lie? Probably not. The tension you see is most likely the result of thinking through a complicated response. One of the many times you can expect to see crossed arms is when a person is focusing on a complex or difficult situation.

Now imagine that you see the same set of nonverbal signals in response to a seemingly simple and straightforward question.

In this context it's more likely that you have hit on a "hot spot" and would want to investigate with some follow-up questions.

Look for Clusters

Nonverbal cues occur in what is called a *gesture cluster*—a group of movements, postures, and actions that reinforce a common point. A single gesture can have several meanings or mean nothing at all, but when you couple that single gesture with other nonverbal signals, the meaning becomes clearer. For example, if you're talking with someone who begins fidgeting, it may not mean much by itself. But if that person is also reducing eye contact and pointing his feet toward the door, there's a very good chance that he's finished with the conversation and wants to leave.

Because they add clarity, clusters play a key role in our ability to spot a liar. Before entering a negotiation, I coach clients to be aware that a good indication of bluffing is when they see three separate body language cues that send duplicate signals of stress, uneasiness, and disengagement. Negotiations are one context in which you should expect a certain amount of bluffing. But if you suspect that your negotiation partner is an out-and-out liar, watch closely for deception signals and get commitments in writing.

According to recent research by David DeSteno of Northeastern University, there is one specific cluster of nonverbal cues that proved statistically to be a highly accurate indicator of deception.[3] The "telltale four" of nonverbal signals associated with lying are: hand touching, face touching, crossing arms, and leaning away.

A person's overall demeanor is far more revealing than any isolated body language signal. So always remember to look for

The Telltale Cluster

groups, or clusters, of behaviors. And when dealing with someone you suspect of lying, watch for the telltale four.

The Best Lie Detectors

Are there people who are naturally better at spotting deception than others? According to the latest research, yes. The expression *You can't kid a kidder* may be literally true. The ability to deceive others and the ability to detect deception have now been linked scientifically by a joint study conducted by the University of London and University College London.[4] In a game called the Deceptive Interaction Task, researchers created the first-ever demonstration proving that skilled liars make good deception detectors.

But that doesn't mean that those who are inclined to trust people are more likely to get duped (which is good news to me because my husband accuses me of being too trusting). A study in which the University of Toronto simulated job interviews found those who agreed with the statement *Most people are basically honest* were better able to distinguish applicants who lied from those who told the truth.[5] The more faith in their fellow human beings they had, the more they wanted to hire the honest interviewees and avoid the lying ones. People who were low in trust were more willing to hire liars and were also less likely to recognize liars.

If you are a woman in business, you also have a slight advantage over your male colleagues in detecting lies—not because you are necessarily more duplicitous or more trusting but because, in general, women listen more attentively, watch people more closely, and are better at picking up subtle nuances and reading body language.

If you are wondering if there are any shortcuts to becoming a better lie detector, the following research published in *Psychological Science*[6] might give you some ideas. The study looked at whether our tendency to mimic the gestures and the facial expressions of people we are speaking with helps us detect when they are lying—but the exact opposite was discovered. When subjects suppressed their inclination to mimic, their ability to spot a lie increased. I suspect this is because *not* mimicking reminds you to remain an objective observer rather than become an empathetic partner.

What Body Language Won't Tell You

You can learn a lot from watching body language in business situations. If you are interviewing a new candidate for a job opening, you can spot signs of stress and gently probe in that area for more details. If you are a supplier negotiating a contract with a key client, you can notice when he frowns, leans back, or abruptly crosses his arms as he reads one part of the contract. You can assume that there is something about that particular clause that causes him concern.

But there are some things that body language won't tell you. From *The Nonverbal Advantage: Secrets and Science of Body Language at Work,* here's one example[7]: Bob works in the office of a district attorney (DA) and often sits next to the DA during trials. He has become adept at reading the body language of jurors and using that knowledge to figure out which jury members are in sync with the state's case and which are going to be tougher to convince.

At a recent murder trial, the prosecutor was questioning her crime scene analyst as a gory set of slides of the victim was being shown. All of the jurors were paying rapt attention to the photos and the investigator's testimony—all the jurors, that is, except one, a macho-looking man who kept turning his head away, as if the photos were unimportant. "That's the guy we're going to have trouble with," Bob predicted. "He's obviously not interested in our evidence." But at the end of the trial, the verdict was unanimous: guilty!

Bob was right on target about the juror's blank stare, head turn, and avoidance of the photos. But what he took for lack of interest was in fact queasiness! When Bob interviewed the juror after the trial, he found out that this big, burly man couldn't stand to look at gruesome crime scene photos.

There may be times when you find yourself in similar circumstances. You accurately pick up emotional cues but misinterpret the motive behind them. As you increase your accuracy in reading expressions and other nonverbal signals (and you'll be a lot better off being aware of these cues than oblivious to them), you will always have to guard against jumping to conclusions about what those signals mean regarding honesty and deceit. Remember: a truthful person's fear of not being believed looks almost identical to a liar's fear of getting caught in the lie.

Detecting Deception through Nonverbal Cues

Reading body language to detect deceit in a business interaction is similar to what a professional poker player does during a card game. The card player is looking for *tells*—nonverbal cues that indicate increased stress or are out sync with what the opposing poker player is saying. The difference is that you are applying these skills in a workplace setting.

There are 30 body language tells that will help hone your liar-spotting skills. It's is a long list, so you don't have to memorize it. But I do recommend that you keep it and the list of verbal cues for future reference. If you read through them a few times, you'll begin to develop an overall sense of the kinds of signals that most often indicate stress, unease, and *possible* deception. I think you'll be surprised at how this added insight automatically comes to mind when you next wonder if someone is telling the truth.

30 Body Language Tells to Hone Your Liar-Spotting Skills

Unusual eye contact. The biggest body language myth about liars is that they avoid eye contact. While some liars do find it difficult to lie while looking you in the eyes (children more often than adults), most practiced liars will deliberately overcompensate by making too much eye contact and holding it too long. Remember too that the "correct" amount of eye contact varies from culture to culture. In the United States, for example, businesspeople are taught to look at each other during conversations. In some other cultures, extended eye contact by a subordinate with his or her manager is considered inappropriate and disrespectful.

Another myth, popularized by Neuro-Linguistic Programming—that looking to the right indicates lying whereas looking to the left suggests truth telling—has also been shown in new research to be false. The University of Edinburgh completed three different studies to show that there was no correlation between the direction of eye movement and whether the subject was telling the truth.[8] There is one eye signal cluster I've observed that often *does* follow a less-than-truthful response, however: after speaking the liar may immediately look down and away and then back at you again in a brief glimpse to see if you bought the falsehood.

Pupil dilation. One nonverbal signal that is almost impossible to fake is pupil dilation. The larger pupil size that nearly all people display when telling a lie can be attributed to an increased amount of tension and concentration.

Change in blink rate. In general, blink rates increase with stress levels. But a unique pattern has been associated with deception: A study at Portsmouth University shows that a person's blink rate slows down as he or she decides to lie and stays low through the lie. Then it increases rapidly (sometimes up to eight times the normal rate) after the lie.[9]

Eye blocks. A sure sign of distress is when someone touches the eyebrows or squeezes the bridge of the nose while closing the eyes. But other eye blocks can be telling, too. When children don't want to look at something, they'll cover their eyes. When adults don't want to face something, they may rub their eyes or close them in an extended blink.

Blushing or blanching. Physiological and impossible to control, both blushing and blanching are caused by the autonomic nervous system and may be triggered by embarrassment, distress, or lying.

Fake smile. It's hard for liars to give a genuine smile while seeking to deceive. Real smiles crinkle the corners of the eyes and change the entire face. Faked smiles involve the mouth only and are often asymmetrical.

Retracted lips. Lip retraction (where lips are compressed and pulled back between the teeth) is a common reaction when people are drawn or maneuvered into a discussion in which they feel they must hold something back.

Duper's delight. A fleeting smile after an untruthful statement often indicates that someone believes he or she has fooled you.

Under- or overproduction of saliva. When the autonomic nervous system downloads a rush of adrenaline, it causes a dry mouth. Watch for sudden swallowing in gulps (saliva overproduction) or the increased need to drink water and to lick or moisten lips.

Nose touching. A real boy's nose may not grow when he tells a lie, but watch closely and you'll notice that when someone is about to lie or make an outrageous statement he'll often unconsciously scratch, rub, or cover his nose. This is most likely because a rush of adrenaline opens the capillaries and makes his nose itch.

Mouth touching. Mouth covering is a common gesture seen in very young children who are being untruthful. Adults have learned to eliminate this giveaway display, but the unconscious urge remains. It is not uncommon to see liars bring a hand to their face to brush the side of the mouth or to touch or even cover one cheek.

Vocal cues. Paralinguistic signals (how you say what you say) that often indicate lying include changes from baseline behavior in tone, which usually rises with stress level as the vocal chords constrict. Another signal is a noticeable slowing down of speech rate, typical of unpracticed liars. And when a liar finally does admit the truth, you may hear the voice drop to a noticeably softer volume.

Clammy palms. When a person is under stress, the arterial vessels constrict, drawing blood into the center of the body. As a result, hands and feet become cold and clammy. Just remember that lots of people have a clammy handshake, and this could be a natural condition. Pay more attention when someone's usually warm hands turn cold.

Foot movements. Because feet are the farthest from your brain, they are the hardest area to control. When lying, people will often display nervousness and anxiety through increased foot movement. Quite unconsciously, people will fidget, shuffle, and wind their feet around each other or around the furniture. They will stretch and curl their feet to relieve tension, rock them from side to side in an effort to self-pacify, or point them toward the door, signaling a desire to exit.

Unusual stillness. Sometimes, in an effort to stop their gestures from giving them away, liars (particularly inveterate ones) will make themselves sit or stand with unnatural stillness. This statue effect is a very useful cue and is most revealing when it is in direct opposition to more-relaxed baseline behaviors. I've seen people freeze midgesture, as they suddenly realize that their body language may be inappropriate.

Pacifying gestures. To ease tension, liars will attempt to soothe themselves with self-pacifying gestures like wringing hands, massaging between the eyes, scratching the back of the head, grabbing the back of the neck, biting a lip, fiddling with jewelry or hair, touching the earlobe, pulling at a collar or loosening a necktie (men), and touching the throat notch at the base of the neck or playing with a necklace (women).

Decreased illustrators. Because liars are less spontaneous than truth-tellers, they use fewer illustrative hand gestures (such as pointing, drawing a picture in the air, or holding their hands apart to show a measurement) to help tell their stories.

Hidden hands. When you see a colleague's hands suddenly plunging into pants pockets or disappearing under the conference table, it may be a sign of discomfort or an indication that the person is trying to hide something.

Nervous laughter. Nervous laughter both relieves stress and appears to mask how much anxiety a person is really feeling. It is also used as a stalling mechanism, giving that little bit of extra time to think and prepare a safe answer. As such, nervous laughter can indicate that the topic under discussion is a hot or critical issue for the speaker and is often a sign of evasiveness or even deception.

Self-pacifying gestures

Frequent and shallow breathing. You may see a liar's chest begin to heave or hear breathlessness in his or her voice.

Throat clearing. Of course, throat clearing can be triggered by many things, but liars clear their throats (and may do so repeatedly) as a result of tension in the neck muscles causing throat restriction.

Cathartic exhale. When liars finally tell the truth, you'll often see them give a sudden and deep exhale. While not particularly helpful in spotting deception as it is occurring, this cue can expose a lie after the fact.

Fidgeting. People fidget even when telling the truth, but liars often try to suppress their fight-or-flight impulses, which results in twitchy movements. Expect to see increased fidgeting as the deceiver feels more and more trapped by the lie.

Gestures after words. When the truth is being spoken, accompanying gestures will automatically precede the words by a fraction of a second. When a lie is being told, gestures may follow the words, like an afterthought—just a beat too late.

Partial shrug. A partial (abridged) shoulder shrug usually indicates that a person lacks confidence and conviction in what he or she is saying.

Torso shield. When a person crosses the arms or uses objects such as a notebook, purse, or folder to cover the chest, it is probably a form of unconscious protection—and the more tightly a shielding object is gripped, the greater the level of discomfort revealed.

Distancing behaviors. Shifting the head or torso—which is especially telling if accompanied by a slight shoulder lean away from you—is often indicative of a distancing behavior. These behaviors reduce the magnitude of emotional connection and nearly always reveal discomfort with whatever has just been said.

Forward lean. In direct contrast but equally telling, the forward lean is a technique more-practiced liars may use to draw you into an almost certainly dubious story.

Foot locks. This is a limbic-brain response analogous to the foot movement cue discussed previously, but it is more critically related to fear and distress. While a person is seated, the ankles cross and pull back under the chair—locking the feet together.

Longer or shorter response time. If you ask a question that should require some thought and the reply is a snap answer, the quick response may be a sign of a planned and rehearsed lie. When prepared, deceivers start their answers more quickly than do truth-tellers. If your question comes as a surprise, however, liars will often take longer than usual to respond—simply because the process of inhibiting the truth and fabricating a lie to replace it is more complicated than answering the question honestly.

Nonverbal cues are easier to detect when the liar has a greater motivation to deceive or when the liar is tired. Both have to do with added cognitive load. When the stakes are high, added pressure makes the liar pay closer attention to making the story sound plausible and not enough attention to possible nonverbal giveaways. When someone is exhausted, he has fewer cognitive resources to give to the mentally taxing process of lying.

Nonverbal cues are more difficult to spot if the liar is sitting behind a desk or other partially concealing object. You'll have greater success judging a person's emotional state when you can see the entire body. You'll also have greater success if you can train your brain to *watch* and *listen* at the same time. Watching and listening simultaneously is more difficult to do than you might think (although I assure you it gets easier with practice), but doing so will allow you to pick up mixed clusters of nonverbal and verbal cues that, processed together, will give you a clearer picture of deceptive intent.

Detecting Deception through Verbal Cues

People's choice of words often reveals more about them than they realize. For example, because most people experience stress when lying, they often try to circumvent that by speaking the literal truth. So, if your boss says, "I'm thinking of recommending you for the position," that is exactly what she means. She has not told you she did recommend you. She has not told you she will recommend you. All she said is that she is thinking about doing so. In the same way, if your colleague states, "That's all I can tell you," believe him. He can't or won't tell you more. But remember: that doesn't mean this is all he knows.

A liar's choice of words, in contrast to a truthful person's, will frequently include several verbal cues.

20 Verbal Cues to Hone Your Liar-Spotting Skills

Unnecessary elaboration. The more someone embroiders a story, adding unnecessary details and irrelevant information, the greater the chance he or she is making it up.

Change of subject. You've just asked your co-worker how his meeting went. He answers, "Good," then abruptly switches the subject to ask about your latest project. He might be keeping the content of the meeting private for any number of reasons, but you'd be right to wonder what he was withholding.

Stalls. Repeating the question, asking that the question be repeated, or asking a question back rather than replying to what was asked—all give the liar extra time to fabricate an answer. Question: "Why did you leave your last job?" Response: "Why did I leave my last job?" or "Why do you think that is important?"

Selective wording. Liars often avoid answering the question exactly as asked. Question: "Have you ever used drugs?" Response: "I don't use drugs." Question: "Did you steal the money from petty cash?" Response: "I wasn't even working that day." In both cases, people replied in a way that seemed to answer the question but didn't. And you still don't know if they've ever used drugs or if they stole the money.

Quasi-denials. Liars may say something that sounds like a denial but isn't: "Do I look like someone who would do that?" instead of "No, I didn't do it." They may even go into attack mode and try to impeach your credibility or competence with questions like "Why are you wasting my time with this stuff?" or "How long have you been doing this job?"

False starts and repetition. Stammering, stuttering, slurring words, false starts, and frequently repeating the same words and phrases—all are signs of a higher cognitive load and the possibility of deception.

Grammatical errors. We all make grammatical errors, but liars often change pronouns and tenses in midsentence. Here's an example of both: "I leave for the office about 8 a.m. every day, and then we stopped for coffee."

Qualifiers. "To the best of my knowledge," "I could be wrong," "You may not believe this, but," "If I recall correctly," and "As far as I know."

Disclaimers. "You won't believe this, but" and "I know this sounds strange, but."

Modifiers. "Not necessarily," "Most of the time," "Hardly ever," and "It depends on how you look at it."

Softeners. When describing a situation, truthful people tend to use assertive, unambiguous words such as "steal," "cheat," or "forge." Liars use softer words like "borrow," "mistake," or "omit" to minimize the act.

Overformality. A liar's language tends to become awkwardly formal and stilted, characterized especially by the avoidance of commonly used contractions. A liar might say, "I did not have sex with that woman, Ms. Lewinsky," rather than, "I didn't have sex with Monica."

Credibility builders. "To tell the truth," "To be honest," "Truthfully," "In all candor," "Honestly," "Frankly," "I swear on my mother's grave," and "I swear to God." Whenever you hear these words or phrases, a warning bell should ring in your brain.

Distancing language. A liar might say, "There were problems with that project," rather than, "We had problems analyzing the results of the employee engagement survey."

Depersonalizing language. Deceivers use fewer self-references ("I," "me") and more generalizations ("everyone," "they," "them"). For example, a liar might say, "The accounting department must have made an error," rather than, "It was my responsibility."

Hesitations. "Uh," "er," "um," "ah."

Guilt-trip statements. Liars make a show of taking offence in the hope that you'll abandon the question while defending yourself. For example, a female liar might say, "I'll bet you aren't hounding any of the men about this. Why is it that you assume only a woman would be guilty?"

Convincing statements. Liars will deflect the question by trying to convince you that nothing in their past would indicate deceit. So the woman in the previous example might add, "Look, I am a hard worker and I have been a good employee here for 10 years. I don't understand why you are treating me this way."

Forward thinking. People who tell the truth tend to jump forward and back in time. Deceivers need to construct their stories in chronological order. Because they are working from a false memory, it is almost impossible for liars to tell their stories in reverse chronological order.

Inadvertent truth. Occasionally, a liar will let the truth slip. I once heard an executive announce to his staff, "I promise you that this restructure will result—I mean, will not result—in massive layoffs."

Researchers at Stanford University studied CEO deception during quarterly earnings conference calls.[10] They found that deceptive bosses made more references to general knowledge ("as you know") and referred less to shareholder value and value creation. They also used more-extreme positive-emotion words; that is, instead of describing something as "good," they called it "fantastic." And deceptive executives avoided the word "I," opting instead for the third person. They also used fewer hesitation words, suggesting that they might have rehearsed or been coached.

Verbal cues are easier to detect if the liar hasn't had time to prepare. A good lie requires rehearsal and memorization. If you suspect deception, it can be helpful to relax people first, to get them to lower their guard, and then encourage them to talk as much as possible. The more they talk, the greater the chance that they'll say something revealing.

Listen carefully to what people are telling you. Stay especially alert if people tell you what they are *not* doing: "I don't want you to take this the wrong way" or "It's not that I have anything to hide." Most often that's a lie. One final word of caution: When you and the person you are dealing with are not from the same culture or don't speak the same native language, it is almost impossible to accurately decipher their verbal and nonverbal cues.

Virtual Liars

Shortly after one of my articles on workplace deception was published, the following comment was posted on my blog: "I once worked with a guy who lied for two years over e-mail about his project knowledge and skills. He was only found out when he started working at headquarters where we could see him in person."

My anonymous correspondent may have been lying, of course (though why, I can't imagine), but that's really the point of the story. There is virtually no way to detect a virtual liar. Or, if there is, it is a far more difficult process.

Communication mediums run a spectrum from lean to rich. A lean medium transmits less information than a rich medium. For example, if you are e-mailing or texting, there is almost nothing that gives added clues to the meaning of what you write. Because they lack visual and auditory social signals, lean mediums are relatively poor transmitters of emotion. A communication channel becomes richer—and hence more helpful in exposing duplicity—as you add human elements. Telephone calls and teleconferences give listeners access to vocal cues. Videoconferencing allows participants to view facial expressions and hand gestures.

With this in mind, I wasn't surprised to read about research at Wichita State University that found that sending text messages leads people to lie more often than they do with other forms of communication.[11] What did surprise me, however, was the study's discovery that people were more honest via video than in the other mediums tested—including face-to-face. When questioned about this unexpected finding, the researchers attributed it to the "spotlight effect," where a person feels they're being watched more closely on video than in person.

On video or in face-to-face encounters, it is our skill as human lie detectors that helps us spot the deceivers and frauds. There is one crucial impediment to our success in doing so, however: it is not our limited detection abilities or the liar's skill, as you might expect, but rather our own unconscious biases and judgments that blind us to otherwise obvious signals of deception in others.

CHAPTER 3

Why We Believe Liars and Play into Their Hands

B ERNARD M ADOFF, MASTER MANIPULATOR AND WORLD-class fraud, bilked thousands of investors out of roughly $20 billion over a period of some 40 years.[1] Have you ever wondered why so many people trusted him for so long?

The answer is simple, really: Like all master frauds, he was totally convincing. He had the right credentials, wore the right clothes, belonged to the right clubs, socialized with the right people, and dropped the right names at the right moments—without appearing to be doing anything more sinister than telling an anecdote about an old friend who just happened to be well positioned and well respected. But just as important as all that, people trusted Madoff because they *wanted* to trust him.

How do I know? Because that's human nature. And anyone who thinks he or she is too sharp to be taken in by a con man like Bernie Madoff had better read this chapter with particular care.

Recognizing that we are being lied to is an important social and business skill. If it were only a matter of paying closer attention to verbal and nonverbal cues, all that we'd require to become polished deception-detectors is in the previous chapter. But it's not that simple. Surprisingly small factors—where we meet people, what they wear, what their voices sound like, whether their posture mimics ours, if they mention the names of people we know or admire—can enhance their credibility to the extent that it actually nullifies our ability to make sound judgments about them. Our own unconscious biases, vanities, desires, and self-deceptions only add to the hijacking of our reason. When we put our faith in a co-worker we don't really know, or hire someone we haven't properly vetted, or give our life savings to a seemingly nice man on the basis of good vibes, we almost always do so for reasons of which we are completely unaware.

Did you know that there are facial features that we innately trust or mistrust? By studying people's reactions to a range of artificially generated faces, researchers in Princeton's Department of Psychology found that faces with high inner eyebrows, pronounced cheekbones, and a wide chin struck people as trustworthy.[2] Conversely, faces with low inner brows, shallow cheekbones, and a thin chin were deemed untrustworthy. Of course, you and I realize that eyebrow shapes and cheekbones have no correlation to truth or deception, but unconsciously we override our rational minds and make an instant and instinctive judgment. We just can't help ourselves.

In another series of experiments, researchers at the Kellogg School of Management used subliminal cues, such as mentioning the name of a good friend, to trigger feelings of trust for a stranger.[3] These studies also showed that a potentially risky decision to trust someone could begin below an individual's conscious awareness—before there has been time to evaluate or verify the subject's track record, for example, or inquire about his reputation.

Lasting Impact of Snap Judgments

Two seconds—30 seconds, tops—is all the time it takes you to assess the confidence, competence, status, likeability, warmth, and, yes, trustworthiness of someone you've just met. In fact, it's impossible *not* to make these snap judgments about people. Human beings are wired that way. Why? Blame it on the limbic brain.

According to the triune brain theory, our gray matter is actually three brains in one: The reptilian brain controls the body's vital functions such as heart rate, breathing, temperature, and balance. The cortical brain handles activities such as language, analysis, and strategizing (the seat of our conscious thought is here in the prefrontal cortex). But it is the limbic brain that is most responsible for the value judgments that strongly influence our reactions and behaviors.

The limbic system, in particular the amygdala, is the first part of the brain to receive information and react to it. The amygdala takes in all incoming stimuli and decides instantly whether it is threatening. Before our conscious mind has had time to evaluate the truthfulness of someone's statement, the limbic brain has already made a decision about the potential threat. Because these decisions are made without conscious deliberation, they affect us with the immediacy and the power of an old-brain survival imperative—unconsidered, unannounced, and in most cases impossible to resist.

We decide whether to trust someone almost immediately after meeting them, and although this first impression can, and often should, be revised, there are powerful psychological forces that prevent us from doing so. Once we are convinced that someone is honest or deceptive, we will go through all sorts of mental gymnastics to reinforce our initial judgment.

We're All Biased

Biases result from the mental shortcuts we unconsciously revert to when facing otherwise overwhelming information-processing demands. For example, in a negotiation we need to carry on a conversation while simultaneously evaluating the risks and the payoffs of the offers coming across the table and making judgments about the person making those offers.

Because few of us have the mental agility to consciously perceive and process all of the factors needed to make such calculations, we rely on estimates—or guesses—based on our past experiences, preconceptions, and biases. While these mental shortcuts work reasonably well most of the time, they also leave us vulnerable to a variety of judgment traps. When faced with a practiced liar, for instance, our usually reliable biases lead us to misidentify or ignore even obvious deception cues—which is precisely what the liar wants us to do.

Whenever we meet new people, our brain automatically and immediately begins to categorize them in some way—male or female, same or different, friend or foe—to predict what is likely to happen next. In 1998 a trio of researchers at the University of Washington introduced a computerized assessment called the Implicit Association Test (IAT), which has become one of the standard tools for measuring the degree to which an individual's unconscious mind categorizes people and automatically assigns certain traits to those categories. The IAT has revolutionized the way social scientists look at stereotyping—as the rule rather than the exception.[4]

When we are deciding whether or not to believe someone, the category we've assigned them to—and our past experiences with others from that group—influences our judgment of deception or truthfulness. So, if we previously worked for a female boss who couldn't be trusted, we are more likely to be suspicious of our current female boss and to look for signs of deception.

Even more insidious, our categories are informed (or misinformed) by what we view in the media. For example, if we are meeting a new team member from a different race or ethnic background than our own, our evaluation of his or her honesty is influenced by the way people from that race or ethnicity are portrayed in the movies or on television and the type of media coverage most associated with them. Research shows that we will react to this influence even when we harbor no conscious prejudice. In fact, one telling finding from the IAT is that there is little correlation between a person's implicit biases and his or her explicit or conscious bias. In fact, some participants told me they were appalled when they viewed their test results—which were diametrically opposed to beliefs they consciously hold.

Biases That Affect Our Ability to Detect Liars

Some of our biases give people the benefit of the doubt. Other biases lead us to be more skeptical of some people and more trusting of others. Here are a few of the biases that can color our perception and cloud our judgment.

Ingroup/outgroup bias. It is far easier for a deception to be successful when the liar and the person being lied to come from the same background or have similar interests. Even relatively small similarities, like rooting for the same sports team or attending the same seminar, can create a bond. That's because of a well-known principle in social psychology that people define themselves in terms of social groupings: any group that people feel part of is an ingroup, and any group that excludes them is an outgroup. We think differently about members in each group and behave differently toward them. Similarities make us feel comfortable. We assume we know what ingroup people are like: they're good people—like us! Differences make us a little wary. When we see people as part of an outgroup—especially if we are also prejudiced against that group—we are more likely to judge any negative act as typical of their character and to attribute any positive actions as the exception.

One of the most significant "experiments" on ingroup/outgroup bias was carried out not in a psychology lab but in the schoolroom of an Iowa teacher, Jane Elliot. In 1968, the day after the assassination of Martin Luther King Jr., Elliot decided to address the issue of racial prejudice by dividing her all-white third-grade class into groups on the basis of eye color. As profiled in the PBS *Frontline* documentary "A Class Divided,"[5] Elliot showed how easy it was to turn some of her seven-year-old pupils into a privileged ingroup by telling them that blue-eyed children were "better." Within minutes the blue-eyed children began to ridicule their unfortunate classmates, calling them "stupid" and shunning them on the playground during recess. And when Elliot then flipped the situation and said that the brown-eyed children were superior, they exacted the same punishments on the blue-eyed students.

Truth bias. The expectation of honesty is another mental shortcut used to bypass the huge clutter of verbal and nonverbal signals that bombard us throughout every conversation. Unless deception is obvious from the start (or unless we have instantly labeled someone as untrustworthy), we focus and fixate on early signs of sincerity and effectively seal ourselves off from conflicting indicators. People who know and like each other are particularly resistant to doubting each other's truthfulness. Often it seems better to accept what we are told by those we trust and depend on than to challenge their truthfulness. We therefore overlook or explain away statements and nonverbal cues that others would automatically find suspicious.

Appropriate-behavior bias. We all have a tendency to make judgments about another person's integrity based on our ideas of appropriate behavior. This shows up in lie detection when we believe that we know how we'd act if we were telling the truth—and that other truthful people would or should behave in the same way. In reality, as discussed in chapter 2, there is no universal behavior that signals deception or honesty. People are individuals with their own unique set of verbal and nonverbal behaviors, which, again, is why establishing a clear baseline is so important when trying to separate truthfulness from deceit.

Confirmation bias. There is a magician's trick called the vanishing-ball illusion, in which a ball tossed in the air seems to disappear—but in reality is never actually thrown. The trick depends on the magician's skill in creating such a strong expectation of the throw that the audience actually hallucinates having seen it. The trick works because we are psychologically programmed to see what we expect to see.

The popular CBS television show *60 Minutes* dramatized confirmation bias with polygraph examiners in a program aired in 1986.[6] The show's staff set up a mock situation in which four polygraph examiners chosen at random from the New York telephone directory were asked to administer polygraph examinations to four different employees of the CBS-owned magazine *Popular Photography,* regarding the theft of camera equipment (when in fact no theft had occurred).

Each of the four examiners was subtly led to believe that one of the people they were going to test was the likely thief. The examiners found the identified candidates—a different one in each case—to be guilty simply because that's what they expected would happen.

Attractiveness bias. Unfair though it may be, and even if we proclaim otherwise, we judge people by their appearance. We automatically assign favorable traits to good-looking people, judging them to be more likeable, competent, and honest than unattractive people.

Baby-face bias. There is one set of facial features—large eyes, plump lips, a round face, and a high, smooth forehead—that make an adult face resemble a young child or baby. Baby-face bias is our innate evaluation of people with these features as being more childlike, submissive, naïve, and trustworthy.

Gender bias. Stanford University communication professor Clifford Nass conducted research to see if students would apply gender stereotypes to computerized voices.[7] In one study, half the subjects were tutored by computers with male voices and half by computers with female voices. When the material being taught was about love and relationships, students rated their female-voiced tutors as having more sophisticated knowledge of the subject than those who had the male-voiced tutors—even though both voices had given identical lessons.

This particular gender bias would make it easier for females to falsify expertise in topics like social psychology and the arts and for males to fake knowledge about subjects like finance and science.

Dominant-side bias. Daniel Casasanto, a psychologist at The New School for Social Research, found that not only did right-handed people associate right with good and left with bad but also that left-handers make the reverse associations.[8] His research also demonstrated that we are actually biased in favor of objects and people located on our preferred side. So, as a right-handed person, when liars sit to my right I may be inclined to view their opinions more favorably.

Techniques of Successful Liars

Lying is interactive. The liar is not speaking into a vacuum but rather to us—intelligent, educated listeners. So why are we so easily fooled? Con men and women are successful because of what they know about human nature—and how they use that knowledge to influence us. While there is nothing sinister about understanding human nature and exerting influence (in fact, it's a business skill worth cultivating), liars use this knowledge to manipulate and deceive. The following are seven techniques used by highly successful deceivers.

Seven Habits of Highly Successful Liars

They mimic us. The extent to which we feel that individuals are similar to ourselves, even on a superficial physical level, has a huge impact on our attitude toward them.

In a recent experiment, volunteers were ostensibly asked for their opinions about a series of advertisements.[9] In some cases, a member of the research team mimicked the body language of the participant, taking care not to be too obvious. (*Mimicking*—or *mirroring*—is a matter of assuming the same postures, gestures, and facial expressions as the person we're conversing with.) A few minutes later, the researcher "accidentally" dropped six pens on the floor. Participants who had been mimicked were two to three times more likely to pick up the pens. The study showed that mimicry increased goodwill toward the researcher in a matter of minutes.

People naturally mimic when they are talking with someone they like or are interested in, subconsciously signaling that they are connected and engaged. When done for the purpose of developing genuine rapport, mirroring can be a powerful lever for positive business relationships. Successful liars, however, use mirroring to trick us into believing they are empathetic when in fact they are anything but. Just remember that regardless of legitimate or deceptive intentions, when a person mirrors us we perceive him or her as significantly more persuasive and honest.

They tell us what we want to hear. "Invest with me and get rich." "If you serve on this committee, you'll hobnob with the company's top executives." "This project will give you the experience and the exposure you need for that next promotion." "You'll only have to work overtime on rare occasions."

Maybe.

Or maybe it's just a less-than-truthful come-on from people who understand that when they tell us exactly what we want to hear, we are more likely to believe them. Consider the following classic story that has become part of American advertising folklore.[10]

Shirley Polykoff was an advertising executive in the 1950s. One of her early accounts was Clairol. To turn the image of dyed blonde hair from its association with brassy, "loose" gals to fresh and confident women, she created a campaign using the girl-next-door type of models and the slogan *Does she or doesn't she? Hair color so natural, only her hairdresser knows for sure.*

The campaign proved to be a big success. But initially the client wasn't sure it would be right for Clairol—that is, until the letters came pouring in. One letter in particular caught the client's attention and was circulated throughout the company: "Thank you for changing my life. My boyfriend, Harold, and I were keeping company for five years but he never wanted to set a date. This made me very nervous. I am 28 and my mother kept saying soon it would be too late for me. Then, I saw a Clairol ad in the subway. I decided to take a chance and dyed my hair blonde, and that is how I am in Bermuda now on my honeymoon with Harold."

When Polykoff retired in 1973, she was one of the highest-paid talents in the industry and a member of the Advertising Hall of Fame. At her retirement party, she reminisced with the assembled executives about the mountain of mail received after the launch of that first campaign, nearly 20 years earlier. "Remember the letter from the girl who got a Bermuda honeymoon by becoming a blonde?" Polykoff asked. Of course they all did. "Well," she said, "I wrote it."

The liar in this example was charming and creative, and the lie was a success story for both Polykoff and Clairol. But that's not always the case. The most destructive liars—those who steal our money or our hearts—also realize that it's easier for us to unquestioningly believe them when they tell us exactly what we hope to hear.

They flatter us. Our susceptibility to flattery stems from a simple desire to feel good about ourselves. Whether we realize it or not, we can be unduly influenced by liars who butter us up with compliments about our intellect, taste in clothing, sense of humor, or personal charm. After all, we reason, they are right about those things, so they are probably just as accurate about everything else they tell us.

They charm us. The term *halo effect,* coined by psychologist Edward L. Thorndike, is a cognitive bias in which our perception of one desirable trait in a person can cause us to judge that person more positively overall.[11] When a con artist is charming (and most of them are), we tend to automatically believe that he or she is also perceptive, candid, and totally on our side.

They do favors for us. In July 2012 GlaxoSmithKline was fined $3 billion for promoting drugs for unapproved uses (an illegal practice called off-label marketing) and for failing to report safety data about a diabetes drug to the Food and Drug Administration. In addition, the company was found guilty of paying kickbacks (or sweeteners, as the British call them) to physicians—including Hawaiian vacations, tickets to high-priced concerts, and millions of dollars for speaking tours. While never stated so bluntly, the kickbacks were to entice doctors to prescribe the company's products.[12]

But it doesn't take an unethical favor or expensive bribe to make us feel indebted to someone. And the payback doesn't have to be stated overtly. A close look at the psychology of relationships reveals that most individuals automatically attempt to keep a mental balance between what they contribute to a relationship and what they get back from it. When someone does even a small favor for us, we feel obligated to reciprocate in some way.

They touch us. Touch is the most primitive and powerful nonverbal signal we experience. Infants deprived of touch have developmental problems physically, psychologically, and emotionally. With adults touch retains its power to affect our feelings.

Casual and brief touches on the shoulder, arm, or hand have a much bigger impact than you might guess.

The expression *That person is an easy touch* refers to the persuasive power of touch. In what has been labeled the *compliance effect,* a number of research studies have found that touch increases the likelihood that people will do what you request. It's also been shown that a subject being touched feels increased trust in and connection with the person who initiates the touch.[13]

They dress the part. Liars realize that their appearance plays a huge role in creating an impression of authority and credibility. The better dressed someone is, the more apt we are to follow their suggestions, even if those suggestions are visual and subtle. One research study shows that a jaywalking man in a business suit will have passersby follow him as he crosses the street—but not so if the same man jaywalks wearing casual attire.[14]

How We Deceive Ourselves

In his book *Why We Lie,* David Livingstone Smith theorizes that the unconscious mind frequently scrambles messages before they reach the conscious mind—and it is this manipulation of information before it reaches awareness that makes self-deception possible.[15]

Unconscious Self-Interest

Brain-imaging studies show that when we have a personal stake in the outcome of any event, our brains automatically include our desires and aspirations in our assessments. The process is called *motivated reasoning,*[16] and it utilizes a different physical pathway in the brain (one that includes parts of the limbic system) than the pathway used when we are objectively analyzing data.

Subliminally, we are all highly susceptible to the power of self-interest. But because motivated reasoning is unconscious, we may sincerely believe that we are making unbiased choices when in fact we are making decisions that are self-serving. So your decision to accept someone at face value may have as much to do with your unconscious self-interest as it does with his or her skill at deception.

Above-Average Syndrome

Many of us hold ourselves in such high esteem that if I ask a group of managers to rate themselves on leadership ability, it's likely they will all consider themselves to be well above the norm. This may be accurate, but more likely it is evidence of a very human phenomenon known as the *above-average syndrome.*

This illusion of superiority causes us to overestimate our positive qualities and abilities and underestimate our negative qualities, relative to others. It makes it easier for us to believe that we are more honest, trustworthy, and candid than most of our co-workers and to believe that our deceptions are relatively minor fibs, misstatements, or honest mistakes.

Impostor Syndrome

The flip side of the above-average syndrome is the *imposter syndrome.* First identified in the late 1970s by researchers at Georgia State University, the condition was attributed primarily (but not exclusively) to smart, capable, high-performing women who suffered from chronic self-doubt.[17]

When I speak at women's conferences, and even when I'm coaching female leaders in their organizations, I notice that most women are reluctant to claim their accomplishments ("Anyone could have done it"), and I see how their body language condenses rather than expands, to nonverbally display a lack of status and confidence.

But for both women and men, the impostor syndrome goes beyond lack of confidence. People feel like frauds—attributing their success to luck, timing, or circumstance; and the fear that others will discover that they have been bluffing through their entire career is very real. When we suffer from this syndrome, we'll give more credence to statements about our shortcomings than about our strengths because we "know" we've deceived others into seeing us as more intelligent and competent than we are.

Disguised Biases

Not only are we all biased but we are so unconscious of the process that our biases often appear in a disguised form. In one study participants evaluated résumés of male and female candidates for the job of police chief (a job which figured to trigger a male preference).[18] The résumés were written so that male applicants excelled in some categories and ranked lower in others. In those cases the evaluators assigned a higher significance to the male applicants' areas of strength and a lower priority to those areas in which the males were weak.

But then the résumés were reversed—written so that the female applicants excelled in the areas where the men previously had. And when the genders' strong and weak areas were reversed, the evaluators' opinion of the importance of those areas was also reversed. The evaluators were clearly making their choices on the basis of gender but were totally unaware of having done so.

The Sting of Rejection

Naomi Eisenberger, a social neuroscience researcher at the University of California, Los Angeles, designed an experiment to find out what goes on in the brain when people feel rejected by others.[19] She had volunteers play a computer game, after which their brains were scanned by fMRI machines. Subjects thought they were playing a ball-tossing game over the Internet with two other people.

About halfway through this game of catch, each subject stopped receiving the ball and the two other players threw the ball only to each other (in reality there were no other human players, only a computer program designed to exclude the test subjects at some point). The neuroscientists then looked to see what was happening in the subjects' brains. When people felt excluded, there was corresponding activity in the dorsal portion of the anterior cingulate cortex—the neural region involved in the "suffering" component of pain. In other words, the feeling of being excluded provoked the same sort of reaction in the brain that physical pain might cause.

The particular relevance of this study to the issue of self-deception is this: When we're working in a group, the mere presence of other participating personalities often makes it difficult to keep a grip on what we truly think as individuals. We're such social beings that just as we instinctively mirror other people's body language, we also mimic their valid and invalid opinions—

often without realizing we're doing so—to avoid the sting of social rejection. To combat this natural tendency to mimic and prematurely agree with others, I advise leaders to encourage constructive conflict in their team meetings, which makes positive disagreement feel more comfortable and safe.

The Ultimate Question: How Much Truth Can We Really Handle?

If we're honest with ourselves, the answer to this question is probably *not that much.* The truth, the whole truth, and nothing but the truth is often too hard to take—and just as often not even wanted. You might think things would be much better if every conversation you ever had were conducted in perfect candor and honesty on both sides. But if that actually happened, I think you'd change your mind fairly quickly. Do you really want to hear a full and truthful answer to "How are you?" from every person you meet? Would it help to know that the receptionist who wishes you a good day actually thinks you're a pompous jerk? The considerate, kindly, or encouraging falsehood delivered for well-intentioned reasons is in fact one of the essential oils in the balm that helps work—and life—move forward a little more smoothly. So too, anthropologists believe, is the instinct for self-deception that has probably been part of our mental makeup since the dawn of history.

It isn't deception as such that we have to combat in our working lives; it's *destructive* deception. In chapter 4 I address some strategies that you can use to do just that.

CHAPTER **4**

How to Deal With Liars

"**WHICH WORKPLACE LIARS ARE YOU MOST GRATEFUL FOR?**"

Audiences are often startled into silence when I pose this question. But after a little encouragement and few minutes' reflection, they begin to come up with some interesting answers:

- "I like liars who say, 'That's a nice jacket' and don't mention the 10 pounds I've gained. What's that—a lie of omission?"

- "I'm grateful for co workers who ask me how my project is going, even if they're just being polite."

- "My team leader tells us what a great job we're doing. We all know it's not the truth, but we try to live up to her expectations."

So, how about you? Which liars—and lies—make your business interactions more pleasant, energizing, and friendly? As you start this chapter about dealing with liars, it's good to remember that not all liars need to be "dealt with." Some, in fact, should be thanked.

But as you already know, not all liars are benevolent. Some spread malicious gossip that can damage reputations and derail careers, some take undue credit and kill team morale, and some lie about behaving unethically or illegally and have a negative impact on the entire organization.

So, how do you deal with *those* liars?

The honest answer is *I don't know*. As much as I'd like to offer a one-size-fits-all formula, I can't—and that's where this chapter comes in. It will help you identify those factors and assess the pros and cons of different courses of action to develop your own strategy in your particular circumstances.

Dealing With Liars in *Your* Workplace

Dealing with liars in the workplace takes a thoughtful and individualized strategy. I don't know the "right answer" for your situation because it depends on how you evaluate a variety of factors.

Six Key Questions to Ask Yourself

Your strategy for dealing with workplace liars depends on how you answer the following six key questions.

Who's the liar? Liars may work with you, report to you, or hold hierarchical power over you. You may be interviewing a liar, negotiating with one, or working with one on the same team. You and the liar may be professional rivals, good friends, or both. Each of these business relationships brings its own level of intimacy, authority, and responsibility that may affect how you decide to proceed.

What is the impact of the lie? Is the lie causing rework or harming the outcome of a project? Is the lie destroying team spirit and collaboration? Is it costing the organization money? Is it damaging the reputation of the company? Is it hurting your or someone else's professional reputation? Could the lie get the wrong person hired or fired? Or is the lie simply annoying?

What is the liar's standing in the organization? Liars may be popular, successful, powerful, and well connected in the organization's hierarchy, or they may be disliked and distrusted. If it came to a your-word-against-his situation (which should always be avoided), who is most likely to be believed?

What's your goal? Do you want the liar to confess or just to know that *you* know? Do you want him or her to change behavior, to apologize, to make retribution, or to face punitive action? And if you achieved that goal, how would it affect your future relationship with the liar?

What's your motive? Why is this important to you? For example, some people tell me:

- "No one should have to live with this abuse."

- "If I come forward, maybe others will do the same."

- "I've always hated that guy, and it just bugs me to have to put up with him!"

What are the possible consequences? You have three choices when dealing with liars:

- You can confront them, directly or indirectly.

- You can report them to your boss or to the human resources department.

- You can ignore them and do nothing.

Each option has both positive and negative consequences. And as you will see in the following section, if you evaluate those potential consequences before you act, you will have a better idea of what you might be facing, whatever action you decide to take.

Strategies for Direct Confrontation

Confronting liars quickly and directly gives you the advantage of catching them before they have time to practice and perfect the lie. It may also give you a sense of personal satisfaction to expose the liar—especially if the lie was malicious or destructive.

Document. If you are going to confront a liar, it's better sooner than later. But do take the time to document every behavior that validates your position and note what you did in response.

Stay calm and professional. State the truth and don't get pulled into any arguments or emotional exchanges.

Ask for what you want. What would satisfy you? An admission? An explanation? An apology? A retraction?

State the consequences. Let the person know that if the lies continue, you will need to discuss the situation with your boss (if you haven't already done so) or file a complaint with the HR department.

Consider bringing a witness. Of course, occasional deceptions from basically honest co-workers can and should be handled personally. But if you are dealing with a master manipulator, you don't want to give him or her the opportunity to say that you were inappropriate or abusive in your confrontation.

Document the meeting. Compare notes with your witness, making sure you both remember events and details in the same way.

Strategies for Indirect Confrontation

Dealing with a liar presents the challenge of possibly having to maintain a business relationship with the perpetrator. If that is the case, an indirect confrontation might serve you better than a direct accusation. This is most effective when your primary objective is to confirm your suspicions or to simply let the liar know that you know the real story.

Indirect confrontation creates a situation in which, to innocent parties, your comments sound innocuous. It's only to the liar that they take on added significance. If you stay alert for verbal and nonverbal signs of stress and deception as people respond, you will most likely see the liar give him- or herself away.

Inquire. Let's say that your boss lies in a meeting and you want to give him a way out; you might approach him privately later and say, "I didn't understand what you just said, but I may not have all the information. Are you sure you meant that?"

Ask a "loaded" question. In a situation where a team member lied to the boss about your work hours, you could say to the deceiver, "I wonder if you could help me. Someone has been telling our manager that I leave the office early every day. Who do you think would say such a thing?"

Start by expressing doubt. If a colleague has taken credit for your idea, you might tell him or her, "I may be wrong, but I thought I heard you say that you created the customer survey."

State the situation. To the person who is spreading rumors about you, ask a rhetorical question: "Isn't it odd that with all the backstabbing going on in this company, people still think it won't get back to the one they're talking about."

Allude. You are interviewing a job candidate whose behavior changes in response to your question about why she left her previous employer. You ask, "Do you still keep in contact with your old boss?" Then, if the stress signals continue, you could be more direct: "Is there any reason why you should be uncomfortable discussing this?"

Ask a one-word question. You are in a negotiation, and your counterpart lies about competing bids. You tilt your head to the side, look him in the eye, and say, "Really?" (then wait for the response).

Request an action. You are in a meeting with your boss, and she alludes to the fact that she is disappointed with your job performance—but omits any meaningful feedback. You stay calm and professional while asking, "What specifically would you like me to do differently?"

Ask for clarification. An HR manager told me how she handles interviewees who she believes lied on their résumés. "We're going to verify everything on your résumé, so let's clear things up now. What specifically needs to be revised so that it's perfectly accurate?"

Ask a final question. Another hiring manager ends all of his interviews with this question: "What haven't I asked you that you think might be a concern if found out later?" He tells me that he is constantly amazed by what people reveal in response, which has included drug use, criminal records, and spousal abuse.

Don't say anything. If you ask someone a question and he or she doesn't answer it to your satisfaction, stay silent. People often feel compelled to fill the gap by providing additional information.

Strategies for Reporting Liars

According to a report by the Ethics Resource Center, most whistleblowers do not initially go outside their company to report wrongdoing.[1] They turn to management first. It's only when people don't trust their company to handle the issue or when they are frustrated by their futile attempts to get an appropriate response from their organization that they go elsewhere.

Reporting liars will bring them to the attention of upper management or, in the case of whistleblowers, to the attention of authorities and sometimes the media. But be aware that when acting as a whistleblower you will probably not be able to protect your own anonymity. This is why you need to be clear on how destructive this liar is and how important it is to you to expose him or her. In very serious cases, whistleblowers need to decide if they want to stay with the organization or if they are willing to leave their employer.

For lesser offences also consider that just because you complain to senior management doesn't mean that the company will take action—or that the action will be what you anticipated. That said, if you do decide to report a serious offence or even a smaller lie, keep the following tips in mind.

Document. Document the lie, its impact, and any action you have taken to date.

Follow procedures. Find out if your organization has written procedures for employees bringing issues to the attention of human resources or upper management. If so, follow them carefully. An employment attorney told me, "In many companies there are particular policies and procedures that provide for an actual duty to report—addressing sins of omission as well as commission—as well as clear direction for reporting an issue up the supervisory chain, including level-skipping in the event that the issue is with a supervisor."

Bring support. When appropriate, get others to join you. In one case where a liar was sabotaging the efforts of a team member, several other teammates went with the complaining employee to validate her concerns in front of their supervisor.

Focus on the business impact. Describe how the liar is jeopardizing the project, reducing productivity, costing the organization money, causing turmoil in the office, or harming the company's reputation.

State your emotions but keep them in check. It's fine to say that you are hurt, angry, or frustrated—but if you whine, shout, or cry, you'll only succeed in losing credibility.

When the Liar Is Your Boss

One office worker told me that her manager would do unethical "favors" for certain staff members—such as padding their timesheets—without telling them in advance. She would then later confide to these "favored" people that "both of us could lose our jobs if anyone found out about this." Eventually, unable to do their work with this threat hanging over their heads, most of the "favored" staff members resigned. Why the manager behaved in this way is anyone's guess, but I'd be willing to bet that her motive was power.

People in powerful positions can get away with lying in ways that people who report to them can't. As the boss, you can be fairly direct with liars; but unless you work for a manager who genuinely encourages candor, confronting your superior carries a risk. Many people in my research, however, reported that it is a risk they felt worth taking:

- "I confronted my team leader about his lying behavior and have since told his boss that this man is extremely economical with the truth."

- "I left the project my boss was managing and told him and human resources exactly why I did."

However you choose to deal with it, when you work for a boss who lies, it is a smart idea to start collecting evidence. For example, if your boss keeps falsely claiming that he told you to do something, ask for written or e-mailed instructions—or follow up each verbal directive with a short note to him, indicating what you understand the directive to be.

I also hear about the *higher-authority ploy,* in which *your* boss blames *his or her* boss for denying your request. Of course, this may really have happened, but too often it is just an easy way to say no without talking personal responsibility. The manager who tells this lie believes that you will simply accept the decision of the higher authority. One savvy employee put an end to this subterfuge when she countered, "What specifically did your boss say when you asked about this?" Asking any suspected liar what someone else said is a good tactic to remember. Deceivers find it more difficult to make up comments from another person.

When the Liar Reports to You

Teri and Mark were always competing for assignments. Teri was the top performer in her department, but Mark was a close second. When Teri heard that Mark was spreading a rumor about her having an affair with the department manager ("the only reason she gets the good assignments"), she immediately reported it to her boss—the manager with whom she was supposedly sleeping.

Teri was offended by the deceitful rumor, but what her manager did next upset her even more—at least initially. Teri waited for him to come to her defense and to directly accuse Mark, but instead he brought them both into his office and said,

"I hear that there is some problem between the two of you. I just want you to know that I can't tolerate this kind of disruption on my team. You need to resolve your issues and get back to the job you were hired to do."

Years later when Teri told me about this incident, she understood and agreed with the indirect approach that her boss had taken. "In a subtle but effective way, Mark got the message. His ego was saved, we continued to work together effectively, and the rumors stopped."

If you are a manager dealing with liars who report to you, your chosen strategy will depend on whether you want to change their behavior and retain them as employees or close the matter by terminating them. That decision, in turn, depends on the severity of the lie and its impact on your team, your projects, and your company—and, of course, on company policy.

When You Want to Retain Someone Who Lied

Manager: "One team leader had selective memory. She retold stories in ways that discredited others and made her look good."

Carol: "How did you know she lied?"

Manager: "It was reported to me, and then I heard her myself."

Carol: "What did you do?"

Manager: "In her performance review, I pointed out the lies and said that that was not acceptable behavior. Then I offered her coaching on how to be more factual, specific, and measurable. I'm hoping she improves."

If you are going to meet with someone who has lied on a relatively minor matter but whom you'd like to retain, here are some general guidelines.

- Document your observations and all of the concerns of the liar's co-workers.

- Decide if you want to confront directly or indirectly: "Why do you keep promising clients that you can deliver results when you know it's not possible in the time frame you quote?" versus "I just got a call from our new client. Is there anything that happened in your meeting with them that I should know about?"

- If you are going to take a more indirect approach in the hopes of drawing someone out, first spend time building rapport. One way to help people relax is to literally get on the same side. Move your chair so that it is next to theirs, stand facing the same direction, or take a walk with them.

- Ask open-ended questions and keep the person talking. The more someone talks, the more likely he or she is to open up. Keep your tone conversational and not accusatory.

- When the employee has admitted the lie, make it clear that such behavior has to stop if the person wants to remain part of your team.

- Then, if appropriate, ask if the employee would like your help, with coaching or training.

One thing to remember about liars who remain on the job is that some really are basically untrustworthy: "This one woman was caught in many lies, but because her lies had no apparent motive or benefit I concluded that she was just compulsive. Still I kept a close eye on her. Eventually, she was caught charging merchandise for herself on the company credit card. She was then allowed to resign."

When You Need to Terminate Someone Who Lied

Manager: "I had a former assistant who lied to get away with activities that were against company policy."

Carol: "How did you know she lied?"

Manager: "Someone reported her—and when I confronted my assistant, she confessed."

Carol: "What did you do?"

Manager: "Remember, I said she was my *former* assistant."

Managing a liar is never an enjoyable task, and removing one from your employment may not be easy either. Some lies are so serious that you really have no other choice. In that case, you need to check your organization's policies and procedures about dismissing someone and follow those steps carefully. Here are some other guidelines for your consideration.

- ■ Document your observations in writing; include all of the concerns and complaints of the liar's co-workers. These notes should be given to human resources to go into the employee's personnel file and should detail exactly what transpired.

■ Confront the person privately.

■ Be candid, respectful, and professional. Keep your emotions in check and your personal opinions to yourself.

■ Be direct. Explain the circumstances and let the
employee know that you have evidence or documenta-
tion of the lies.

■ Remind the liar (if accurate) that the behavior is a
violation of the organization's code of ethics—or give
any other reason why his or her employment must
be terminated.

■ Let the employee know what will happen next—what
his or her rights and responsibilities are as a discharged
employee.

■ Talk with your team. Although you can't legally go
into any details about the firing, you can set the record
straight and let your employees know that the person
has been let go or asked to resign.

Getting a Confession

Sometimes you have substantial evidence of a lie. Other times
the evidence may be weaker, and your goal is to get the liar to
confess. In those cases, you'll need to ask a series of questions
and to employ all of your lie detection skills from chapter 2 as
you observe the person's responses. Remember that a single
deceptive indicator may mean nothing, but clusters of verbal

and nonverbal cues should get your attention—and encourage you to dig deeper.

Let's say you believe that Stephen stole a company laptop computer. You could start with one of the following:

- "Stephen, what do you know about the missing laptop?"

- "Did you take one of our laptops home last night?"

- "I know that you borrowed the laptop. I just need to know why you did so without asking permission."

Sometimes this kind of direct confrontation is all that's needed either to get an admission or to observe guilt. But if not, you could try a more indirect approach:

- "Is there any reason why someone would report seeing you with the missing laptop last evening?"

- "What do you think should happen to the person who stole the laptop?"

Remember to stay alert for the "convincing" statements liars use: "I am a loyal employee." "I have a great reputation." "I would never jeopardize my job by doing something like that."

You can neutralize those statements by acknowledging or agreeing with them: "I know you have been a loyal employee. You've had consistently good performance reviews." Then go right back to your questioning: "I really need to talk with you about the missing laptop. Where is it now?" You know that a statement like "I would never jeopardize my job by doing something like that" doesn't directly answer the question "Did you steal the laptop?"

If You Choose to Do Nothing

There may be circumstances in which you have a moral obligation to report the liar. In some instances there is a statutory duty to report, such as in cases of child pornography, child abuse, and sexual harassment, particularly for certain professions such as teachers and healthcare workers. It's best to check with your HR department or an attorney so that you know the law in this regard.

But more often, you do have a choice, and at times you may choose to do nothing. Regardless of whether you are dealing with the lies of a subordinate, a colleague, or your manager, doing nothing, at least initially, gives you the chance to think things over and get your emotions under control. On the other hand, delaying too long also gives the liar more time to continue spreading misinformation or otherwise behaving badly. If you are the manager, it may also appear to others that, by your silence, you are condoning the deception. Still, in some cases you'll decide that dealing with a particular liar is just not worth the effort. It's good advice to choose your battles strategically.

Deciding to do nothing, however, doesn't mean that the liar is forgiven. That is a separate decision. As one still-annoyed team member told me about another: "I didn't do anything, but I didn't forget about the lie. I will never trust him, and I will never help him."

Doing nothing also buys you time to see how the situation plays out: "One of my staff members wanted my job and belittled my performance, saying that he knew more than I did. As it turns out, the guy was also downloading porn at work, so I didn't have to do anything. My boss fired him. I was fine with that."

One More Liar to Deal With

In what the *New York Times* calls "one of the most bewildering recent journalistic frauds," Jonah Lehrer, author of the best-selling book *Imagine: How Creativity Works,* admitted to fabricating quotes from Bob Dylan.[2]

The fabrications cost Lehrer his job as a staff writer for the *New Yorker.* In addition *Imagine,* which had sold more than 200,000 copies in hardcover and e-book, was pulled from distribution.

In a statement released through his publisher, Lehrer apologized: "The lies are over now," he said. "I understand the gravity of my position. I want to apologize to everyone I have let down, especially my editors and readers."

We lie for all sorts of reasons. Some of our lies, like Lehrer's, make no sense to others. Why would a successful writer and well-paid lecture circuit speaker jeopardize his reputation and career for a few made-up quotes? And how in the world did he think he could get away with it?

This brings me back to the last liar with whom we all have to deal: ourselves. From a falsified résumé to embezzlement, all lies have consequences. Major lies, when discovered, have major consequences, and even small lies over time can result in hurt feelings, anger, and distrust. The following are a few thoughts for your consideration.

Consider your motives for lying. Are you lying to protect others? Are you lying to hurt others? Are you lying because you don't know another way of refusing to do something? Are you lying to make yourself look better?

Consider the consequences of your lying. If the lie is believed, what impact will it have on other people? This is important to consider with all lies but crucial if the lie is about a colleague's behavior with child pornography, child abuse, or any other illegal activity that could destroy a falsely accused person's career. If your lie is discovered, how will it affect your career and business relationships? Is it worth the risk?

Consider the alternatives. What is a truthful but considerate way to deal with the situations in which you lie? For example, if you lie to avoid doing things you don't want to do, how could you refuse to do something in a more direct but polite and assertive way?

Consider what a slippery slope deception is. Once you catch yourself thinking, It's no big deal or Everybody's doing it (I call this the Lance Armstrong defense), be aware that you are rationalizing your own dishonesty.

⸺ 🤞 ⸺

Now consider this: When you look at yourself in the mirror each morning, you know in your heart that you are looking at someone whose word others can rely on, who is trustworthy and candid in all the ways that matter. But do your fellow workers see you in that way, too? Does your boss? What about those new guys watching you from across the room? And the client you've been trying so hard to impress—what does she really think of you?

Time to look at the next chapter.

CHAPTER 5

Do You Look Like a Liar?

SOME YEARS AGO I RECEIVED A PHONE CALL FROM A NEW York business executive who asked if I could coach him about a problem he was unable to resolve on his own.

The problem was that despite all of his widely acknowledged abilities and accomplishments, this gifted man was consistently passed over for promotion by senior management. Why? Because along with being brilliant, he was also shy, soft-spoken, gentle, and naturally self-effacing— qualities that made him a joy to work with but which were misidentified by C-suite executives as withdrawn, withholding, uncertain, insincere, and even deceptive.

Could I coach him? Of course I could.

Did we have a happy ending? Of course we did because, in this client's case, it was easy. After our first session he realized that his advancement was being sabotaged by a variety of unconscious gestures, postures, and speech mannerisms. By our third and final session, he had made key behavioral changes without in any way changing who he was fundamentally, and he was finally getting the positive attention of senior leaders.

This client was only one in a long line of men and women whom I've helped do battle with the potentially damaging consequences of being misread by colleagues and superiors. At the heart of nearly all such battles are two basic facts: First, emotionally charged situations—a job interview, for example, or a meeting with senior executives—are stressful and make us behave in ways of which we're not entirely aware. Second, we are poor judges of the impression we make on others. Seeing ourselves on video for the first time often makes both points quite clearly. I remember the shocked reaction of another client I was helping through interview jitters when I played back the practice job interview I'd recorded: "Hell, *I* wouldn't hire me," he declared. "I look like a liar!"

What about you? When you are feeling shy, stressed, or intimidated, do the signals you send get misdiagnosed as deception? Is there something in your posture, demeanor, or voice that robs you of your credibility and makes others instinctively distrust you or disregard your opinion? If so, is there anything you can do to change those false impressions?

This chapter is all about *impression management*. It offers tips to help you project your true competence and confidence—and to ensure that feeling anxious, introverted, or awkward in stressful situations doesn't inadvertently signal untrustworthiness or deceit.

Why Others Get the Wrong Impression

This chapter concentrates on techniques to reinforce people's positive perceptions of you, but it is important to emphasize here that however carefully you prepare, misinterpretations will occur.

You can expect people to read your body language incorrectly when they don't know the context or haven't had time to become familiar with your baseline. And because you can't control the way other people's judgments are influenced by their conscious and unconscious biases, it's always a good idea to note their reactions and be prepared to modify your behavior on the spot when required.

Context. You already know that you can't make sense of someone else's behavior unless you understand the circumstances—the context, the backstory—governing it; but your colleagues won't always have this insight. You may be slouching because you're tired, but people who don't know this will likely read your posture as boredom or a lack of interest. You may be more comfortable standing with your arms folded across your chest, but others see you as resistant or not forthcoming. If, because you don't know what else to do with them, you keep your hands stiffly by your side or stuffed into your pockets, you can give the impression that you're insecure or deceptive—even if you are neither. And when you fidget, stammer, or display other stress signals for any reason, people won't know that reason and may instead assume that you are hiding something or simply lying.

Baseline. You also know that one of the keys to accurately reading body language is to compare someone's nonverbal response to their baseline, or normal, behavior. But if people haven't observed you over time, they have little basis for that comparison.

This is especially important to remember when meeting people for the first time. Your staff may know that you habitually scowl when you are concentrating, but that new client won't.

(You may not know it yourself, unless a friend or coach has pointed it out.) When the new client sees you scowling, she will most likely think that something is wrong—and you may see her morph from a new client to an ex-client right before your eyes.

Biases. Everyone harbors hidden biases and prejudices that influence the unconscious judgments they make. Reactions based on biases are instinctive, and none of us has much, if any, control over them. Some of these biases may work unexpectedly in your favor—the mere shape of your face or the resemblance of your voice to one fondly remembered may earn you all sorts of unlooked-for credibility. Other biases, however, may and often do work against you. For example: if that remembered voice that is so similar to yours triggers emotional memories of fear or disgust, it may take continued effort on your part to overcome the suspicion and the mistrust that it has triggered.

People will also assess your credibility and honesty through an array of cultural biases. These may range from seemingly inconsequential behaviors—such as how close you stand to a colleague in conversation, how much or little you touch others, the degree of emotion you display, the kind of hand gestures you use—to occasionally more-obvious prejudices involving education, language, religion, gender, age, and ethnicity.

Projecting Confidence, Competence, and Credibility

We are all instinctively drawn toward people who believe in themselves—or who at least look like they do. The simple truth is, when you look confident, you are judged to be competent and credible. When you look unsure of yourself, your credibility—and even your basic honesty—may be questioned.

If you are naturally upbeat, confident, and charismatic—and if you never feel shy, introverted, anxious, or intimidated—you won't need the following tips. But if you are very sure of yourself in some situations and less so in others (like I am), here are 20 ways you can overcome that situational shyness or nervousness and project your genuine confidence, competence, and credibility.

20 Ways to Project Genuine Confidence, Competence, and Credibility

Stand tall and take up space. Power, status, and confidence are nonverbally displayed through the use of height and space. Keeping your posture erect, your shoulders back, and your head held high makes you look sure of yourself.

If you stand you will look more powerful and assured to those who are seated. If you move around, the additional space you take up adds to that impression. If you are sitting, you can look more confident by putting both feet flat on the floor, widening your arms away from your body (or hooking one elbow on the back of your chair), and spreading out your belongings on the conference table to claim more territory.

Widen your stance. When you stand with your feet close together, you can seem hesitant or unsure of what you are saying. But when you widen your stance, relax your knees, and center your weight in your lower body, you look more solid and confident.

Lower your vocal pitch. In the workplace the quality of your voice can be a deciding factor in how you are perceived. Speakers with higher-pitched voices are judged to be less truthful, less empathetic, less powerful, and more nervous than speakers with lower-pitched voices. One easy technique I learned from a speech therapist was to put your lips together and say, "Um hum, um hum, um hum." Doing so relaxes your voice into its optimal pitch. This is especially helpful before you get on an important phone call, where the sound of your voice is so critical.

Speakers who speak slowly are also judged to be less truthful, less persuasive, and more passive than people who speak faster. To project confidence and competence, modulate your pitch and volume, minimize your noticeable pauses, and speak a little faster and a little louder.

Can people really change their natural speaking style?

Sometimes.

Take the case of Margaret Hilda Roberts, who in 1959 was elected as a Conservative member of Parliament for north London. She had political ambitions, but her voice was a problem—too high pitched, too "schoolmarmish." She learned to lower her pitch and speak with more authority—and she did pretty well for herself. She changed her last name after marrying a wealthy businessman, and in 1979 Margaret Thatcher became the first female British prime minister.

Become a Method actor. Trying to display confidence when you're actually feeling tentative, or trying to be perceived as upbeat and positive when (for any reason) you are feeling the opposite, is a tricky thing to pull off. Here's a technique, adapted from Lee

Strasberg's and Constantin Stanislavski's Method acting, which draws on emotional memories: Think of a past success that fills you with pride and confidence. (This doesn't have to be taken from your professional life—although I do encourage clients to keep a "success log" so that they can easily find such an event.) Then picture that past success clearly in your mind. Recall the feeling of certainty, of clarity of purpose, of accomplishment—and remember or imagine how you looked and sounded. Recalling that genuine emotion will help you embody it as you enter the meeting room or walk to the podium.

Strike a power pose. Research into the effects of body posture on confidence, conducted at Harvard and Columbia Business Schools, has shown that simply holding your body in expansive, "high-power" poses (leaning back with hands behind the head and feet up on a desk, or standing with legs and arms stretched wide) for as little as two minutes stimulates higher levels of testosterone—the hormone linked to power and dominance—and lower levels of cortisol, a stress hormone.[1]

Try this before your next important business meeting, and I guarantee you will look and feel more confident and certain. In addition to causing hormonal shifts in both men and women, these poses lead to increased feelings of power and a higher tolerance for risk. The study also corroborated my observation that people are more often influenced by how they feel about you than by what you're saying.

Maintain positive eye contact. You may be an introvert, you may be shy, or your cultural background may have taught you that extended eye contact with a superior is not appropriate, but businesspeople from the United States, Europe, Australia, and many other parts of the world will expect you to maintain eye contact 50 to 60 percent of the time.

You and I know that a lack of eye contact is not necessarily a sign of lying, but it is still the most commonly believed myth, so it has to be acknowledged. If you continually look down (which is often a signal of submission), let your eyes dart around the room, or otherwise avoid meeting the other person's gaze, people will probably think that you don't believe what you are saying or that you are being deceptive. Here's a simple technique to improve eye contact: whenever you greet a business colleague, look into his or her eyes long enough to notice what color they are.

Talk with your hands. Brain imaging has shown that a region called Broca's area, which is important for speech production, is active not only when we're talking but also when we wave our hands. Because gesture is integrally linked to speech, gesturing as you talk can actually power up your thinking. Whenever I encourage clients to incorporate gestures into their deliveries, I find that their verbal content improves, their speech is less hesitant, and their use of fillers ("um" and "uh") decreases. Experiment with this and you'll find that the physical act of gesturing helps you form clearer thoughts and speak in tighter sentences with more-declarative language.

Use open gestures. Keeping your movements relaxed, using open arm gestures and showing the palms of your hands—the ultimate See? I have nothing to hide gesture—are silent signals of credibility and candor. Individuals with open gestures are perceived more positively and are more persuasive than those with closed gestures (arms crossed or hands hidden or held close to the body). Also, if you hold your arms at waist level and gesture within that plane, most audiences will perceive you as assured and credible.

Try a steeple. You see lecturers, politicians, and executives use this hand gesture when they are quite certain about a point they are making. This power signal is where your hands make a "steeple"—where the tips of your fingers touch, but the palms are separated. When you want to project conviction and sincerity about a point you're making, try steepling.

Manage your stress. Stress from any source can cause you to tense up and display the same signs of anxiety that alert people to a possible liar. Although there are a variety of ways to reduce stress—from exercise to meditation—I suggest this one-minute stress reliever: Sit with your weight evenly distributed on both feet and sitz bones. Look straight ahead with your chin level to the floor and relax your throat. Take several deep belly breaths. Count slowly to six as you inhale. Hold your breath and increase the tension in your body by making fists and tensing the muscles in your arms torso and legs. Then, as you exhale, allow your hands, arms, and body to release and relax. When dealing with on-the-spot tension during a tricky interview or negotiation, try clenching your toes and localizing your stress (unseen) in your feet.

Mirror. We like and trust people who are similar to us. The importance of this simple fact is something that liars know all too well—and employ all too often—but that truthful people sometimes forget. When liars mirror (subtly mimic the facial expressions, posture, and gestures of the person to whom they are speaking), it's in the hope of making their deceptions believable. When you are being truthful, mirroring others will build rapport, making you more persuasive, and enhancing the (accurate) perception that you are empathetic and honest.

Remove barriers. Using props as barriers makes it look as if you need protection or are hiding something. Move your laptop, purse, briefcase, or anything else on your desk that could create a barricade between you and the person you're talking to. Better still, come out from behind the desk and sit beside him or her. Remember what we know about someone's preferred side: if you sit on the right side of a right-handed colleague, your ideas will be given added credibility.

Use your shoulders and torso. Face people directly when speaking to them. Even a quarter turn away gives the impression that you are disengaged or not interested in what's being discussed. (At that point, if your body language is saying "uninterested" but your words are maintaining the opposite, you will be perceived as a liar.)

Reduce nervous gestures. When we're nervous or stressed, we all pacify with some form of self-touching, nonverbal behavior—rub our hands together, bounce our feet, drum our fingers on the desk, play with our jewelry, twirl our hair, fidget—and when we do any of these things, we immediately rob our statements of credibility. If you catch yourself indulging in any of these behaviors, take a deep breath and steady yourself by placing your feet firmly on the floor and your hands palms-down in your lap or on the table. Stillness sends a message that you're calm and confident.

Keep your voice down. This tip is especially applicable to females in business. Women's voices often rise at the ends of sentences, as if they're asking a question or asking for approval. When stating an opinion, be sure to use the authoritative arc, in which the voice starts on one note, rises in pitch through the sentence, and drops back down at the end.

Smile. Smiles have a powerful effect on us. The human brain prefers happy faces, and we can spot a smile at 300 feet—the length of a football field. Smiling not only stimulates your own sense of well-being but also tells those around you that you are approachable and trustworthy.

Research from Duke University proves that we like and remember those who smile at us—and shows why we find them more memorable.[2] Using functional magnetic resonance imaging, the Duke researchers found that the orbitofrontal cortices (a "reward center" in the brain) were more active when subjects were learning and recalling the names of smiling individuals.

Most importantly, smiling directly influences how other people respond to you. When you smile at someone, they almost always smile in return. And because facial expressions trigger corresponding feelings, the smile you get back actually changes that person's emotional state in a positive way.

Curb your enthusiasm. A certain amount of movement and animation adds passion and meaning to a message, but when you express the entire spectrum of emotions you will be viewed not as passionate but as erratic (and possibly out of control). In situations where you want to maximize your authority, it's important to minimize your movements. When you appear calm and contained, you look more powerful and confident.

Perfect your handshake. It's worth devoting time to cultivating a professional shake—remember that touch is the most powerful and primitive nonverbal cue. The right handshake can give you instant credibility, and the wrong one can cost you a job or a contract. So, no "dead fish" or "bone-crusher" grips, please. The first makes you appear to be a wimp, and the second signals that you are a bully.

Handshake behavior has cultural variations, but the ideal handshake in North America means facing the other person squarely; making firm, palm-to-palm contact, with the web of your hand (the skin between the thumb and first finger) touching the web of the other person's hand; and matching hand pressure as closely as possible without compromising your own idea of a proper professional grip.

A great handshake is important for all professionals, but it is especially key for women, whose confidence is evaluated by the quality of their handshake even more than it is with their male counterparts.

Watch your fillers. As mentioned, speech fillers are superfluous sounds or words, like "um" and "you know." Today I hear fillers more and more in the business world. The CEO of a Silicon Valley startup recently said to his team, "So, I, ah, passionately believe that we have an opportunity to, uh, you know, um, take this technology to a new level. So we just, uh, need to, ah, go for it." He wanted to sound motivational, but his fillers made his message fall flat.

When you hear yourself using fillers, simply stop and pause to give your mind time to search for the next word. You'll sound so much more confident, credible, and motivational when you do.

Remember: it's a balance. In the aptly titled article "Brilliant but Cruel," Harvard business school professor Teresa Amabile points out an important challenge for impression management.[3] The problem is that we often see competence and warmth as being negatively related—warm individuals don't appear as intelligent or skilled as those who are more negative and mean, and tough individuals are judged as far less likable. If you want to optimize your body language to appear at your most charismatic, confident, and credible best, remember to balance power and status cues with warmth and empathy.

Aren't These Tips a Bit Deceitful?

It's a question I am asked all the time: "If I use these body language tips to impress people, aren't I being manipulative and inauthentic?" The answer I always give is, "Yes—and no."

Yes, of course, you're being manipulative—just as manipulative as when you "dress for success" in preparation for a job interview or when you mind your table manners when dining with a client, spell-check your report before sending it to the boss, or rehearse your talking points before a presentation.

And, no, you are not being inauthentic. Rather, you are aligning people's impression of you with your best and most authentic self. You really are intelligent, confident, competent, and trustworthy—right?

Here's an example of how one little signal can block people from seeing the real you—and how making a small change can send a powerful and positive message. It's an e-mail I received from Tracy Finneman, a member of the leadership team at the North Dakota Department of Commerce:

> A few years ago, I became very interested in trust and its importance in the workplace. As a first step, I participated in a 360-degree trust audit. When the results of the review came back, I was surprised to see that my two superiors had given me rather low scores in the area of creating transparency. When I asked for an explanation, I was even more surprised to be told that both felt that I sometimes gave the impression of having a hidden agenda.
>
> I certainly don't have any hidden agendas at work, and it bothered me to think that my co-workers might believe I was somehow being deliberately secretive in my dealings with them. My primary supervisor suggested I try declaring my intent in greater detail before laying out new ideas or plans, and I worked on this quite diligently for the next several months. But when I received my trust audit scores a year later, they were exactly the same, again with this emphasis on a lack of transparency.
>
> It was shortly after this that I attended one of your seminars on body language and began thinking about the vital connection between creating trust and physically

opening up to others. And I wondered if there was something in my body language that gave the impression I had a hidden agenda. Then it occurred to me: My normal, core temperature is lower than most people's. I'm someone who is chronically cold and goes about with my arms crossed for warmth. If it's true people believe what your body says more than the words you use, then my body was communicating something very different from my verbal openness about new ideas and opportunity. For the next several months I made a point of wearing more layers of clothing and of opening my arms and gesturing more generously when speaking.

The result: My latest trust scores showed a significant improvement in my ability to create transparency. All because my body language was now in better alignment with my verbal message.

Tracy is by nature honest and responsible. It really did bother her that the leadership team felt she was not being entirely open with them, and it was a great relief to her when she was finally able to correct that misunderstanding.

But some of you may wonder why she went to all that effort. You may even be thinking, *What good is honesty, openness, and readiness to cooperate with others in the current economic climate?*

Read on...

CHAPTER 6

Reducing Lies in the Workplace

ONE OF MY MOST FREQUENTLY REQUESTED SEMINAR TOPICS today deals with the power of collaborative leadership. Why? Because there is a perception shared by more and more business executives that if they want their organizations to continue to thrive in the global marketplace, they must replace traditional, top-down, command-and-control leadership structures with more-inclusive, "silo-busting" networks to tap the collective wisdom, experience, and creativity of the entire workforce.

The key to making that essential shift is *knowledge sharing,* and the key to knowledge sharing is trust—which brings me back to the subject of this book: lying. As you already know, trust and lying cannot coexist.

Trust is the belief or confidence that one party has in the reliability and the integrity of another—the confidence that one's faith in the other will be honored in return. Dishonesty destroys trust. Once you discover you've been lied to, trust simply vanishes—more often than not forever. And with it goes the very foundation for collaboration.

When trust is low, suspicious and cynical employees view knowledge sharing as weakening their personal power base; meanwhile their leaders, despite lip service to the contrary, follow a need-to-know communication policy, withholding details and insights that are crucial to informed collaboration. As a result, an immense volume of problem-solving capacity is lost to business enterprises every day. Companies are wasting the brainpower that could save billions; or lead to the discovery of a revolutionary new process or product; or, in the current economic climate, help keep them afloat when others are sinking. At the same time, individuals are losing the opportunity to work in the kind of collaborative environment that energizes teams, unleashes creativity, and makes working together both productive and joyful.

By contrast, when trust is high, employees and leaders are more likely to look beyond their individual agendas and functional silos to connect with the whole community in the pursuit of larger organizational goals.

If you are an executive, manager, supervisor, or team leader, this chapter is especially for you. It offers a variety of ideas for reducing lies in the workplace, but many of these suggestions take time, energy, and continued monitoring to implement. I want you to consider upfront why it may be well worth that effort.

Responses from Survey Participants

The final question I put to the 547 business professionals I surveyed for this project was: *How do you feel lying in your organization could be reduced?* I mentioned earlier that 67 percent responded that their senior managers didn't always tell the truth, 53 percent said that their manager lied to them, and 51 percent reported dealing with deceptive colleagues. What I didn't mention before is that about 20 percent of the respondents described their own workplace as an overall high-deception, low-trust environment. Here's a typical comment: "I was not a liar at all until I started working for a company with a toxic senior management team. It is common knowledge that they tell lies about their own schedules (working from home, showing up late, taking long lunches). Now I think it's only fair that I do the same."

It was from this relative minority that I got the most troubling comments about what caused lying as well as the most telling suggestions for dealing with it. The following are the five most representative of those suggestions—all of which, it's worth noting, singled out the policies and the actions of leaders and all of which I advocate.

Five Suggestions for Reducing Lies in the Workplace

Give us honest leaders to follow. "Everything starts with leadership. When there is mistrust in an organization, it starts at the top. Honest leaders reduce the likelihood of others lying. Otherwise, people are driven by fear and backbiting and lies take over."

"Make honesty an implicit value and communicate it clearly, but remember that it will mean nothing unless leaders also model and demonstrate truthfulness. We're not blind. We see everything they do, and all-too-often we follow their bad example."

Focus on finding solutions rather than on placing blame. "People should be made to feel okay about making mistakes because everyone does from time to time. Then we wouldn't feel threatened and need to lie to cover up the mistake."

"We need a culture that accepts mistakes. Make it safe to fail publicly."

"Management should provide sufficient resources (people, budget, time) to actually do the job required. Then we wouldn't have to make up excuses for not reaching deadlines."

Eliminate policies that create liars. "Why can't employees take a 'mental health day'? Why make them lie about it?"

"I've been in human resources for 25 years. If employees have an incentive program that promotes one type of behavior—say approving mortgages even if the applicant pool is high risk—then their actions will follow that incentive."

"Managers shouldn't say they want honest feedback unless they really do. Have you ever tried telling your boss the bad news? I did once and I'm still suffering the repercussions."

Treat employees fairly and equitably. "We need continuous goal-oriented discussions to make sure people are on the same track. Why make us guess—and then berate us when we get it wrong?"

"No favoritism by managers. The minute we saw how the boss plays favorites, we all felt pressured to 'suck up.'"

"Have a no-tolerance policy about liars. Don't hire yes-people in the first place, don't hire people who lie on their résumé, and do fire liars—even when they are senior executives or top performers. That would send a welcome message to the rest of us."

"Each employee, whatever his position, has to take personal responsibility for being truthful, but leaders should give extra encouragement to those farther down the ladder so they'll feel safe about speaking up honestly."

Communicate, communicate, communicate. "Unless there is a specific reason for not sharing information, employees should be told everything. Management keeps announcing new 'transparency initiatives,' but none of them will stand a chance until we dump the need-to-know communication mentality."

"Everybody already knows what's going on, and when management refuses to acknowledge that the rumors are true, it causes employees to continually distrust them. And at town hall meetings, leaders should say, 'I can't answer at this time,' rather than making up a story. Why do they have to lie? It's insulting."

"We need better, more open communication from the leadership team. Actually...we need better leaders."

—⚹—

The most depressing finding in my research was that many of those who identified themselves as working in toxic environments were pessimistic about the likelihood of its ever improving:

"Lying is part of how we do business."

"I've given up. Hopefully, I will be able to escape one day. There are too many liars here. Things will never change."

"Executives lie because of money, politics, power, and a feeble attempt to promote morale. This is just how it is. They try to manipulate us because they don't trust us with the facts."

"Work for yourself. It's the only way you won't be lied to."

Research on What Reduces Lying

As you might imagine, there isn't a lot of research on what really reduces lying, but what there is may surprise you. While not directly applicable to most business environments, this section summarizes what scientists found when they set out to discover if recalling childhood memories, believing in God, seeing a poster of staring eyes, being reminded of moral codes, or receiving higher pay would lessen duplicitous behavior.

Childhood Memories

In a series of experiments at Harvard University, participants were found to be more likely to help the researchers with an extra task, judge unethical behavior more harshly, and donate money to charity when they had actively remembered their childhood.[1] The scientists believe that childhood memories include subliminal feelings of innocence—a frame of mind that positively influences ethical behavior.

Belief in God

According to research, a belief in God doesn't deter a person from cheating on a test—unless that God is seen as a mean, punishing one. In fact, psychology researchers at the University of Oregon and the University of British Columbia found that undergraduate college students who believe in a caring, forgiving God are more likely to cheat.[2]

Big Brother

A group of scientists at Newcastle University conducted a field study experiment demonstrating that merely hanging up posters of staring human eyes is enough to inhibit bad behavior.[3] The research took place in the university's main cafeteria, where people's "littering behavior" was recorded. It was found that during the days when diners encountered posters with pictures of staring eyes (instead of images of flowers) twice as many people cleaned up after themselves. When they hung the staring eyes above an honesty box—where psychology professors and staff were to pay for their tea and coffee—the big-brother effect produced nearly three times as much money.

Moral Code

Dan Ariely and his colleagues at the University of California, Los Angeles engaged a group of 450 participants and asked half of them to recall the Ten Commandments and the other half to recall 10 books that they had read in high school. Among the group that recalled the books, researchers saw the typical widespread moderate cheating. But in the group that was asked to recall the Ten Commandments, there was no cheating whatsoever. When the researchers reran the test, this time asking students to remember the school's honor code, they got identical results. Even when they asked a group of atheists to swear on a Bible, the same no-cheating behavior was observed. Ariely's conclusion is that reminding people of morality, right at the point when they are making a decision, has a positive effect on their honesty.[4]

Higher Pay

Paying employees more makes them less likely to pilfer shelves or rob the till, according to a study of retail workers at 250 convenience stores in 31 large chains.[5] The findings empirically illustrate how higher wages can help reinforce employees' honesty and ethical standards. The researchers also found that 40 percent of that higher compensation could be made up by savings from the reduced theft. They concluded that, taking into account side effects such as reduced employee turnover and new-hire training costs, companies could break even or potentially show a net gain by paying their employees more.

Increasing Workplace Honesty Begins with 10 Questions

In *The Leadership Challenge,* James Kouzes and Barry Posner point out how important honesty is in a leader and how it ranks first among employee expectations, surpassing even competence: "In every survey we conducted, honesty was selected more often than any other leadership characteristic."[6]

It's one thing to understand that honesty and trust start at the top and quite another to develop the strategies and the philosophies that make that understanding a reality. Because every leader, every team, and every organization is unique, there is no one-size-fits-all strategy for decreasing deception and increasing candor in *your* team.

10 Questions to Ask Yourself as You Create Your Own Plan

What do you expect of the people who report to you? "Pygmalion in the Classroom," one of the most controversial articles in the history of educational research, shows how a teacher's expectations can motivate student achievement.[7] This classic study gave prospective teachers a list of students who had been identified as "high achievers." The teachers were told to expect remarkable results from those students, and at the end of the year those students did indeed have sharp increases in their test scores.

In reality, the children were not high achievers but had been chosen at random from the entire pool of pupils. It was the teachers' belief in their potential that was responsible for their exceptional results—a belief that was communicated not directly (the students were never told they were high achievers) but subliminally through positive behaviors such as facial expressions, gestures, touch, and spatial relationships.

In much the same way, a leader's expectations of employees' potential can play a key role in determining how well they perform at work. This effect was described by J. Sterling Livingston in his 1969 *Harvard Business Review* article "Pygmalion in Management": "The way managers treat their subordinates is subtly influenced by what they expect of them."[8]

So, again, the first question to ask yourself is: *What do I expect of my team, staff, or workforce?* If you expect people to communicate with honesty, integrity and truthfulness, you've automatically increased the odds that they will do just that.

Have you covered the basics? Charles A. Lynch is chair of Market Value Partners Company, a management, mentor, and adviser resource for existing and emerging businesses. He has been chair or CEO of a number of major companies, including Saga Corporation and DHL. Listening to Lynch is like taking a course in Leadership 101:

I've worked with a broad cross-section of companies—and I know that you are only as good as the people around you. At heart I'm a fundamentalist. I believe that you need to have everyone focused on and in agreement with an overall mission and a three-year strategic plan. Then you have to make sure that each individual clearly understands his or her quantifiable one-year objectives—that those six to eight key objectives are clearly articulated, written down, and agreed to—and that there is no overlap in responsibility. After that, everyone can write their own performance review because it is obvious when people did or did not reach the goals. And if they didn't—we can discuss why not and what needs to change. It all becomes transparent and upfront.[9]

When you have a foundation like this in place, you lessen the chances of the misunderstandings and the miscommunications that cause people to cover up, make excuses, and lie.

Are your words in alignment with your actions and body language? Whenever your actions are in direct opposition to your statements, you confuse and demoralize your staff and look like a liar—as this e-mail I received illustrates:

My boss drives us crazy with her mixed messages. She says things like, "You are always welcome in my office" and "You are all a valued part of the team." At the same time, she is constantly showing how unimportant we are to her. She never makes eye contact, will shuffle papers when others talk, writes e-mails while we answer her questions, and generally does not give her full attention. In fact, we don't even get her half attention. Then she wonders why we've stopped believing anything she tells us.

If you want people to believe that you want and value their honest opinions, give them your full attention. Don't multitask while they talk. Avoid the temptation to check your text messages, check your watch, or check out your golf swing. (This actually happened: whenever the boss lost interest in a conversation, he would stand, address an imaginary golf ball, and practice his swing.) Instead focus on those who are speaking by turning your head and torso to face them directly and by making eye contact. Leaning forward is another nonverbal way to show you're engaged and paying attention. In cultures of candor, it's important to tell people that they are a valued part of the team. It's even more important to *treat* them that way.

Do you encourage constructive conflict? Samuel Goldwyn, the fabled American film producer, once reportedly said, "I don't want any yes-men around me. I want them to tell me the truth, even if it costs them their jobs."

Goldwyn's comment underscores the concern that even if a leader asks for dissenting opinions, most employees—especially at lower levels of the organization—find it difficult and uncomfortable to speak up. They're unsure whether the leader genuinely wants to deal with conflict, and they fear ridicule or retaliation for "being negative."

In fact, to meet social needs (acceptance and approval), people in any group find it psychologically difficult to go against the majority. As a result, too many people sit in meetings and keep silent, or they gloss over the effect a given proposal will have on their department or co-workers. They wait quietly while the leader proceeds as if everyone is aligned, but this "consensus" is not real. Later, in off-the-record conversations, these same folks may undercut or sabotage the proposal. Rather than discourage resistance and negativity, leaders should surround themselves with people who can debate passionately and honestly before a decision is made—and then unite behind the final decision.

Here are a few ideas to help you get started:

- Assign someone on your team to the role of devil's advocate—to deliberately argue the contrary position as a means of stimulating debate.

- Ask part of the group to think like the firm's competitors (or customers or employees) to bring out and expose flaws in a set of core assumptions.

- Establish ground rules that will stimulate task-oriented disagreement yet minimize interpersonal conflict.

- Keep the proceedings transparent by making decisions based on what goes on in the meeting rather than on behind-the-scenes maneuvering.

- Make sure that team members represent a diversity of thinking styles, skill levels, and backgrounds. If they don't, invite people with various points of view to offer their perspectives.

- Start out with a question and don't voice an opinion. Once you've said, "Here's what I'm thinking..." you have already influenced the team.

Charles Lynch told me that his goal for executive team meetings was to make them open, candid, and constructive. People were treated as equals—and critique was encouraged—with one caveat: "Tell me whenever you think we're on the wrong track, but offer a possible solution when you do."[10]

Do you optimize the power of "nice"? Linda Kaplan Thaler and Robin Koval are chair and CEO, respectively, of Publicis Kaplan Thaler, one of the fastest-growing ad agencies in the United States. Small acts of niceness are the themes of best-selling books co-authored by Kaplan Thaler and Koval and are reflective of their agency's philosophy that "little things and niceness do make a difference."

Here are a few of their tips for creating an atmosphere of trust in which people are more likely to tell the truth:

- Let people know it's okay to have a "stupid" idea or to ask a "dumb" question. In fact, it's desirable.

- Let people know it's okay to bring their "whole selves" (personal idiosyncrasies and issues) to work.

- Praise people for being open and honest and minimize criticism for small missteps.

- Credit the entire team for a successful result.

- If you, as the leader, make an error, own up to it in front of the group.

- If it's true (as it is with Publicis Kaplan Thaler), let people know that failure isn't fatal—that they won't lose their jobs if they make a well-intentioned mistake.

- Try a "yes sandwich." Here is an example of how Kaplan Thaler and Koval dealt with a situation in which one of their creative groups didn't meet client expectations. You can get the general idea of why this is an effective way to get people to face the truth while staying truthful, professional, and *nice:*

Yes: "You are a valuable part of this company, and the client held you in especially high esteem and looked forward to working with you."

Problem: "But in the last three meetings you have disappointed them. This can't continue or you'll lose the assignment."

Yes: "Because you are so talented and capable, we have total faith in you to make the needed corrections and to do the right thing in the future."[11]

Do you know what your culture feels like? Organizational culture is like a hologram: every part contains enough information in condensed form to describe the whole. An observer can see the whole organization's culture and ways of doing business by watching one individual—whether a frontline employee, the receptionist at the front desk, or a senior manager—because there is consistency and predictability to their behavior. Here's how Kaplan Thaler and Koval put it: "Culture is something people experience—that they *sense* as soon as they set foot in your lobby—and not a set of values posted on the wall."[12]

Cultures of candor are achieved through a combination of clearly expressed expectations of acceptable behavior and the ongoing example of leaders (at all levels) who align their actions with those expectations.

The next time you walk into work, ask yourself: *What does this company culture feel like? What would a visitor sense about this culture based on the actions and the attitudes of the first three people he or she might encounter?*

Do you help your team learn from failure? The general manager of an insurance company, concerned that his salespeople were so afraid of failure that they hesitated to take even well-calculated risks, took action at a sales meeting. He put two $100 bills on the table and related his most recent failure along with the lesson he had learned from it. He then challenged anyone else at the meeting to relate a bigger failure and "win" the $200. When no one spoke up, the manager scooped up the money and said that he would repeat his offer at each monthly sales meeting. From the second month on, he never again got to keep the $200. As people began to admit and discuss their failures, the sales department became more successful, quadrupling its earnings in a single year.

One of the drivers of employee dishonesty is the fear of the consequences of failure. For that reason it can be difficult for people in an organization to have a genuine discussion about failure that doesn't include rationalizing, blaming, or lying. Creating circumstances in which it is okay to fail in the context of doing one's best causes deception to dissipate.

To facilitate a more productive conversation about failure, the US Army developed after-action reviews (AARs), which are now used by organizations around the world to help employees learn from their mistakes, prevent future errors, and find new solutions to problems. Basically, the AAR process assembles people who were involved in a planned project or event and asks them to answer these questions:

- ▓ What was the desired outcome?

- ▓ What was the actual outcome?

- ▓ Why were there differences between what we wanted and what we achieved? (Here we are looking for systemic problems.)

- ▓ What did we learn? (What would we do differently next time?)

Do you know who works for you? As I interviewed people for this book, I found that many employees felt compelled to lie (act as if nothing is wrong) when facing personal issues and concerns. I also found that when employees are actively encouraged to bring their whole selves to work—to feel free to actually be who they are, personal problems and all—the resultant sense of acceptance and support can result in higher morale, higher levels of truthfulness, and higher productivity. The following is one such example.

At a claims office of about 125 employees, the head of human resources spent the day observing the local manager. Not only had the office ranked high on productivity but this particular manager had received fantastic feedback on her company's leadership measurement survey. The HR executive was curious to watch her interact with employees to figure out what generated this great response.

As they walked through the office, conversing about the normal work conditions, the manager would often stop and refer to specific individuals: "Steve over there has been in our area for 15 years. Steve also coaches Little League. They won their game last Thursday."

Then they'd move on to someone else, and as they left that person's area, quietly the manager would say, "Sally had some problems with her daughter this year. You know how difficult teenagers can be. We've had many sessions behind closed doors where Sally's trying to sort through these challenges."

Months later when I interviewed the HR executive, that day at the claims office was still etched in her mind. "It became apparent to me," she explained, "that this manager knew all of her people. And I don't mean just knew their jobs: she knew them as individuals—their backgrounds and hobbies, what their concerns were, what got them excited. She knew when they were upbeat because things were going well, and she knew when they were struggling and needed her time and attention. I asked her how on earth she could do this for 125 people. Her response: 'That's my job.'"

Are you seen as vulnerable? Self-disclosure is one of the hallmarks of close relationships, the essence of personal candor and of trust in the other party. Showing your strengths is easy, but full self-disclosure—where you reveal your vulnerabilities and weaknesses—feels more risky.

It may be a risk worth taking. Leaders who combine strength with vulnerability can bond a team faster than any management "technique" I've seen. Here are three leaders and their views on vulnerability:

Robert Burnside, chief learning officer, Ketchum. I accept two things as a leader: First, I am in the spotlight whether I like it or not. And, because I'm in a senior leadership role, it's proper for people to discuss how I'm doing. And second, if I can articulate my strengths and weaknesses to the organization, I believe that people will understand me as a leader who has integrity, who is trustworthy, and who will trust them—because I haven't positioned myself as some perfect being with all the answers. By making myself vulnerable in this way, I'm saying to people: "I'm a human being and I'm willing to hear from you how I might improve." I think that's very effective.[13]

Robert L. Dilenschneider, president and chief executive officer, The Dilenschneider Group. Leaders have to be strong. They have to demonstrate by example that they have the skill (ability) and the will (desire) to do the job. If you have both the skill and the will, then, as a leader, you can afford to be vulnerable. And if you do it properly, it will inspire people around you to pick up those parts of the challenge you're not prepared to deal with. I've seen that work in company after company. It's really all about team building. So, in that way, a leader can make his or her vulnerability a real asset.[14]

Joan Crockett, former senior vice president of human resources at Allstate Insurance Company. Years ago, when Jerry Choate was our CEO, he stood up in front of a room full of people for a speech that was being broadcast throughout the organization. He told a story about how his mother had influenced him and what inspired him. Then he talked about his biggest fear. He said he was afraid that he could let us down. He said that by not being the right kind of leader, he knew he could negatively impact not only employees but ultimately the families of employees. And that's what kept him awake at night.

I've got to tell you, the feedback about that presentation was so powerful and meaningful that it startled me. I anticipated that the speech would get a positive reaction, but I was overwhelmed at the response. For Jerry to speak of what frightened him most—and to express that level of genuine concern for each individual in the company—was extraordinarily compelling to our employees. That one speech did more for pulling our company together, for spring boarding us into productivity goals and high levels of performance, than a hundred "motivational" talks ever could. That's what a leader has to be able to do. You have to be willing to reveal yourself.[15]

Whom do you trust? Getting people to place their trust in you is a matter of always doing what you say you'll do. One thing I've learned over the years is that leaders can talk until they're blue in the face, but they will never create trust unless their *sustained* behavior parallels what they say. This is why building deep trust takes so long. There has to be consistency over time. If your personal leadership style is to be candid but transparency is unusual in your organization, people may automatically believe that you have another agenda. It will take time for them to realize that—with you—what they see is what they get.

But trust is a two-way street. It's not enough that people trust you. You also have to trust them. And I'm not just talking about trusting those you like and agree with; I mean making trust a hallmark of how you deal with every member of your team. Here's what one department head told me:

> I have a deeply and fundamentally positive attitude about the worthiness of people to bring their very best to whatever challenge is at hand. It's not that I assume everybody's right

all the time, but I always begin with the rock-solid belief that everybody has a point of view that's worth hearing. Trust has to do with assuming that the other person has value to contribute, even before they've proven it. That's the core—the belief that people have value and that they are going to come up with good answers. Unless I think that I can run my 1,000-person organization all by myself, I have to trust. I see trust as being highly practical.

Summing Up

Lying in the workplace becomes pervasive—and damaging to trust, collaboration, and productivity—when leaders create an environment that encourages or tolerates it. The strategy for reducing lies is actually quite simple:

- Acknowledge, reward, and promote honesty.

- Don't hire liars.

- Openly share what you know—unless there is a valid reason not to.

- Don't tell people that you "don't know" when you do know.

- Do what you say you'll do.

- Don't set expectations that can't be met.

- Involve people in decisions that affect them.

- Don't pretend to solicit dissenting opinions if you've already made a decision.

- Watch that your body language is aligned with your words.

- Make sure that each team member is crystal clear about what is expected of him or her.

- Foster constructive conflict.

- Take the risk of showing vulnerability.

- Expect people to be trustworthy.

- Eliminate policies that force honest people to lie.

- Learn from failure without placing blame.

- Fire destructive liars, regardless of who they are.

- Be a role model.

- Be nice.

- Tell the truth.

See? Simple!

I never said it was easy though.

So there it is—the answer to that question I threw at you way back in chapter 1: Yes, it might be simpler and more productive if everyone in the organization were upfront and totally honest in all of their dealings with all of their associates all of the time.

But that isn't going to happen.

Ever.

And if some all-seeing, all-knowing ghost of companies present visited you in your dreams one night and said: "Hey, guess what! There isn't one single liar in your entire organization!" you'd probably think he was lying—and you'd be right to. Because lying, as we've seen, is one of the core strategies human beings have evolved over the millennia to deal with the complexities of a largely chaotic, unpredictable, and sometimes threatening life.

But if it's that hardwired psychologically, nothing can be done about it, right? Wrong. As chapter 6 shows, in an emotionally congenial, high-trust environment, where thinking you have to protect or defend yourself happens less and less frequently, the most destructive kinds of workplace lies diminish with startling rapidity, leaving the kindly, well-intentioned "social lies" greater and greater scope to do their good work.

Notes

CHAPTER 1
Liars at Work

1. David Livingstone Smith, *Why We Lie: The Evolutionary Roots of Deception and the Unconscious Mind* (New York: St. Martin's Griffin, 2007).

2. Victoria Talwar and Kang Lee, "Social and Cognitive Correlates of Children's Lying Behavior," *Child Development* 79, no. 4 (2008): 866–81. doi:10.1111/j.1467-8624.2008.01164.x.

3. Edward S. Petry, Amanda E. Mujica, and Dianne M. Vickery, "Sources and Consequences of Workplace Pressure: Increasing the Risk of Unethical and Illegal Business Practices," *Business and Society Review* 99, no. 1 (1998): 25–30. doi:10.1111/0045-3609.00004.

4. Anna Dreber and Magnus Johannesson, "Gender Differences in Deception," *ScienceDirect* 99 (2008): 197–99, http://www.ped.fas.harvard.edu/publications/PEDpublications/2008/Gender.pdf (accessed January 8, 2013).

5. Yasmin Anwar, "Upper Class More Likely to Be Scofflaws Due to Greed, Study Finds," *UC Berkeley News Center,* February 27, 2012,

http://newscenter.berkeley.edu/2012/02/27/greed (accessed January 8, 2013).

6. Genyue Fu, Kang Lee, Catherine Ann Cameron, and Fen Xu, "Chinese and Canadian Adults' Categorization and Evaluation of Lie- and Truth-Telling about Prosocial and Antisocial Behaviors," *Journal of Cross-Cultural Psychology* 32, no. 6 (2001): 720–27. doi:10.1177/00220 22101032006005.

7. Hee Sun Park and Ji Young Ahn, "Cultural Differences in Judgment of Truthful and Deceptive Messages," *Western Journal of Communication* 71, no. 4 (2007): 294–315.

8. Sharon Jayson, "Study Finds That Avoiding Lies Can Improve Your Health," *USA Today,* August 4, 2012, http://www.usatoday.com/news/health/story/2012-08-04/honesty-beneficial-to-health/56782648/1 (accessed January 8, 2013).

9. Zoë Chance, Michael I. Norton, Francesca Gino, and Dan Ariely, "Temporal View of the Costs and Benefits of Self-Deception," *Proceedings of the National Academy of Sciences of the United States of America* (March 7, 2011). doi:10.1073/pnas.1010658108.

10. Tom Pennington and Ron T. Ennis, "RadioShack CEO Resigns amid Resume Questions," *USA Today,* February 20, 2006, http://usatoday30.usatoday.com/money/industries/retail/2006-02-20-radioshack-ceo_x.htm (accessed January 8, 2013).

11. John W. Fountain with Edward Wong, "Notre Dame Coach Resigns after 5 Days and a Few Lies," *New York Times,* December 15, 2001, http://www.nytimes.com/2001/12/15/sports/notre-dame-coach-resigns-after-5-days-and-a-few-lies.html?pagewanted=all (accessed January 8, 2013).

12. Kara Swisher, "Exclusive: Yahoo's Thompson Out; Levinsohn In; Board Settlement with Loeb Nears Completion," *All Things Digital,* May 13, 2012, http://allthingsd.com/20120513/exclusive-yahoos-thompson-out-levinsohn-in-board-settlement-with-loeb-nears-completion (accessed January 8, 2013).

13. Association of Certified Fraud Examiners, "Report to the Nations on Occupational Fraud and Abuse" (2012), www.acfe.com/rttn.aspx (accessed January 8, 2013).

14. Azam Ahmed and Ben Protess, "As Libor Fault-Finding Grows, It Is Now Every Bank for Itself," *New York Times,* August 5, 2012, http://dealbook.nytimes.com/2012/08/05/banks-in-libor-inquiry-are-said-to-be-trying-to-spread-blame/?emc=eta1 (accessed January 8, 2013).

CHAPTER **2**

Deception Detection: 50 Ways to Spot a Liar

1. Charlotte Hsu, "Can a Machine Tell When You're Lying? Research Suggests the Answer Is 'Yes,'" news release, March 26, 2012, http://www.buffalo.edu/news/13302 (accessed January 8, 2013).

2. Paul Ekman, *Emotions Revealed* (New York: Owl Books, 2003), 1–16.

3. Wray Herbert, "How to Spot a Scoundrel: Fidgeting and Trust," *Association for Psychological Science* (blog), April 26, 2012, http://www.psychologicalscience.org/index.php/news/were-only-human/how-to-spot-a-scoundrel-fidgeting-and-trust.html#.UIgnCoWAFao (accessed January 8, 2013).

4. Travis Riddle, "Liars: It Takes One to Know One," *Scientific American,* July 24, 2012, http://www.scientificamerican.com/article.cfm?id=liars-it-takes-one-to-know-one (accessed January 8, 2013).

5. Nancy L. Carter and J. Mark Weber, "Not Pollyannas: Higher Generalized Trust Predicts Lie Detection Ability," *Social Psychological and Personality Science* 1, no. 3 (2010): 274–79. doi:10.1177/1948550609360261.

6. M. Stel, E. van Dijk, and E. Olivier, "You Want to Know the Truth? Then Don't Mimic!," *Psychological Science* 20, no. 6 (2009): 693–99. doi:10.1111/j.1467-9280.2009.02350.x.

7. Carol Kinsey Goman, *The Nonverbal Advantage: Secrets and Science of Body Language at Work* (San Francisco: Berrett-Koehler, 2008), 60.

8. Richard Wiseman, Caroline Watt, Leanne ten Brinke, Stephen Porter, Sara-Louise Couper, and Calum Rankin, "The Eyes Don't Have It: Lie Detection and Neuro-Linguistic Programming," *PLoS ONE* 7, no. 7 (2012): e40259. doi:10.1371/journal.pone.0040259.

9. Sharon Leal and Aldert Vrij, "Blinking during and after Lying," *Journal of Nonverbal Behavior* 32, no. 4 (2008): 187–94. doi:10.1007/s10919 -008-0051-0.

10. David F. Larcker and Anastasia A. Zakolyukina, "Detecting Deceptive Discussions in Conference Calls," *Journal of Accounting Research* 50, no. 2 (2012): 495–540. doi:10.2139/ssrn.1572705.

11. "People Lie More When Texting, Study Finds," *ScienceDaily*, news release, January 26, 2012, http://www.sciencedaily.com/releases/ 2012/01/120125131120.htm (accessed January 8, 2013).

CHAPTER **3**

Why We Believe Liars and Play into Their Hands

1. "Bernie Madoff's Multibillion-Dollar Fraud Began as Far Back as the Early 1970s, Prosecutors Said," *Daily News,* October 2, 2012, http:// www.nydailynews.com/new-york/madoff-fraud-began-back-early -1970s-prosecutors-article-1.1172536 (accessed January 8, 2013).

2. "How Does Another Person's Face Guide Us to Fear or Trust?," *TS-Si News Service,* August 6, 2008, http://ts-si.org/neuroscience/3398 -how-does-another-persons-face-guide-us-to-fear-or-trust (accessed January 8, 2013). To see how computer-generated faces morph from trustworthy to untrustworthy, go to http://webscript.princeton .edu/~tlab/demonstrations (accessed January 8, 2013).

3. Denise Gellene, "A Trusted Name: Why We Trust People We Do Not Know," *Kellogg Insight,* June 2011, http://insight.kellogg.northwestern .edu/index.php/m/article/a_trusted_name (accessed January 8, 2013).

4. Anthony G. Greenwald, Debbie E. McGhee, and Jordan L. Schwartz, "Measuring Individual Differences in Implicit Cognition: The Implicit Association Test," *Journal of Personality and Social Psychology* 74, no. 6 (1998): 1464–80, http://www.citeulike.org/user/ninna/article/2904836 (accessed January 8, 2013). To assess your own biases, Harvard University's Project Implicit has an online IAT demonstration test at https:// implicit.harvard.edu/implicit/demo (accessed January 8, 2013).

5. William Peters and Charlie Cobb, "A Class Divided," *Frontline* (PBS television), originally aired March 26, 1985, http://www.pbs.org/wgbh/ pages/frontline/video/flv/generic.html?s=frolo2p66&continuous=1 (accessed January 8, 2013).

6. "Classic CBS *60 Minutes* Exposé on the Polygraph," AntiPolygraph.org News (blog), January 30, 2007, https://antipolygraph.org/blog/?p=110 (accessed January 8, 2013).

7. Clifford Nass, Youngme Moon, and Nancy Green, "Are Computers Gender-Neutral? Gender Stereotypic Responses to Computers," *Journal of Applied Social Psychology* 27, no. 10 (1997): 864–76, http://www .academia.edu/909183/Are_computers_gender-neutral_Gender_stereo typic_responses_to_computers (accessed January 8, 2013).

8. "The Right Side of Cognitive Science: Daniel Casasanto Explores How the Body Shapes the Mind," *The New School News,* January 23, 2012, http://blogs.newschool.edu/news/2012/01/the-right-side-of-cognitive -science-daniel-casasanto (accessed January 8, 2013).

9. Benedict Carey, "You Remind Me of Me," *New York Times,* February 12, 2008, http://www.nytimes.com/2008/02/12/health/12mimic .html?pagewanted=print&_r=0 (accessed January 8, 2013).

10. "Ms. Shirley Polykoff," *zoominfo*, http://www.zoominfo.com/#!search/profile/person?personId=51866348&targetid=profile (accessed January 8, 2013).

11. "Halo effect," Wikipedia, http://en.wikipedia.org/wiki/Halo_effect (accessed January 15, 2013).

12. Jeanne Whalen, Devlin Barrett, and Peter Loftus, "Glaxo in $3 Billion Settlement," *Wall Street Journal*, July 3, 2012, http://online.wsj.com/article/SB10001424052702304299704577502642401041730.html (accessed January 8, 2013).

13. Judee K. Burgoon, Joseph B. Walther, and E. James Baesler, "Interpretations, Evaluations, and Consequences of Interpersonal Touch," *Human Communication Research* 19, no. 2 (1992): 237–63. doi:10.1111/j.1468-2958.1992.tb00301.x.

14. Monroe Lefkowitz, Robert R. Blake, and Jane Srygley Mouton, "Status Factors in Pedestrian Violation of Traffic Signals," *Journal of Abnormal and Social Psychology* 51, no. 3 (1955): 704–6.

15. David Livingstone Smith, *Why We Lie: The Evolutionary Roots of Deception and the Unconscious Mind* (New York: St. Martin's Griffin, 2007).

16. Chris Mooney, "What Is Motivated Reasoning? How Does It Work? Dan Kahan Answers," *Discover*, May 5, 2011, http://blogs.discovermagazine.com/intersection/2011/05/05/what-is-motivated-reasoning-how-does-it-work-dan-kahan-answers (accessed January 8, 2013).

17. Satoshi Kanazawa and Kaja Perina, "Why Do So Many Women Experience the 'Imposter Syndrome'?," *Psychology Today*, December 13, 2009, http://www.psychologytoday.com/blog/the-scientific-fundamentalist/200912/why-do-so-many-women-experience-the-imposter-syndrome (accessed January 8, 2013).

18. Eric Luis Uhlmann and Geoffrey L. Cohen, "Constructed Criteria: Redefining Merit to Justify Discrimination," *Psychological Science* 16, no. 6 (2005): 474–80. doi:10.1111/j.0956-7976.2005.01559.

19. Naomi I. Eisenberger, Matthew D. Lieberman, and Kipling D. Williams, "Does Rejection Hurt? An fMRI Study of Social Exclusion," *Science* 302, no. 5643 (2003): 290–92. doi:10.1126/science.1089134.

CHAPTER 4
How to Deal With Liars

1. Ethics Resource Center, "Inside the Mind of a Whistleblower" (2012), http://www.ethics.org/nbes/files/reportingFinal.pdf (accessed January 8, 2013).

2. Julie Bosman, "Jonah Lehrer Resigns from *The New Yorker* after Making Up Dylan Quotes for His Book," *New York Times,* July 30, 2012, http://mediadecoder.blogs.nytimes.com/2012/07/30/jonah-lehrer-resigns-from-new-yorker-after-making-up-dylan-quotes-for-his-book (accessed January 8, 2013).

CHAPTER 5
Do You Look Like a Liar?

1. Dana R. Carney, Amy J. C. Cuddy, and Andy J. Yap, "Power Posing: Brief Nonverbal Displays Affect Neuroendocrine Levels and Risk Tolerance," *Psychological Science* 21, no. 10 (2010): 1363–68. doi:10.1177/0956797610383437.

2. Takashi Tsukiura and Roberto Cabeza, "Orbitofrontal and Hippocampal Contributions to Memory for Face-Name Associations: The Rewarding Power of a Smile," *Neuropsychologia* 46, no. 9 (2008): 2310–19. doi:10.1016/j.neuropsychologia.2008.03.013.

3. Teresa M. Amabile, "Brilliant but Cruel: Perceptions of Negative Evaluators," *Journal of Experimental Social Psychology* 19, no. 2 (1983): 146–56. doi:10.1016/0022-1031(83)90034-3.

CHAPTER **6**
Reducing Lies in the Workplace

1. Francesca Gino and Sreedhari D. Desai, "Memory Lane and Morality: How Childhood Memories Promote Prosocial Behavior," *Journal of Personality and Social Psychology* 104, no. 4 (2012): 743–58. doi:10.1037/a0026565.

2. "Different Views of God May Influence Academic Cheating," *ScienceDaily,* news release, April 21, 2011, http://www.sciencedaily.com/releases/2011/04/110420112334.htm (accessed January 8, 2013).

3. Max Ernest-Jones, Daniel Nettle, and Melissa Bateson, "Effects of Eye Images on Everyday Cooperative Behavior: A Field Experiment," *Evolution and Human Behavior* 32, no. 3 (2010): 172–78. doi:10.1016/j.evolhumbehav.2010.10.006.

4. Dan Ariely, *The (Honest) Truth about Dishonesty: How We Lie to Everyone—Especially Ourselves* (New York: HarperCollins, 2012), 39–44.

5. Clara Xiaoling Chen and Tatiana Sandino, "Can Wages Buy Honesty? The Relationship between Relative Wages and Employee Theft," *Journal of Accounting Research* 50, no. 4 (2012). doi:10.1111/j.1475-679X.2012.00456.x.

6. James M. Kouzes and Barry Z. Posner, *The Leadership Challenge* (Jossey-Bass, 1987), 16–17.

7. Robert Rosenthal and Lenore Jacobson, "Pygmalion in the Classroom," *Urban Review* 3, no. 1 (1968): 16–20. doi:10.1007/BF02322211.

8. J. Sterling Livingston, "Pygmalion in Management," *Harvard Business Review,* January 2003, http://hbr.org/2003/01/pygmalion-in -management/ar/1 (accessed January 28, 2013).

9. Charles A. Lynch, phone interview with the author, September 4, 2012.

10. Ibid.

11. Linda Kaplan Thaler and Robin Koval, phone interview with the author, August 9, 2012.

12. Ibid.

13. Carol Kinsey Goman, *"This Isn't the Company I Joined": How to Lead in a Business Turned Upside Down* (Berkeley: KCS, 2004), 154–55.

14. Ibid, 156.

15. Ibid, 155–56.

Acknowledgments

FIRST AND FOREMOST, I WANT TO THANK GEORGE KIMBALL for (once again) being the person I rely on to review each chapter as I write. This book would not have been possible without his guidance and editorial assistance.

I am grateful to Pat Welch of Chameleon Design for his wonderful illustrations. (I rely on his creativity for all of my promotional materials, too.)

I appreciate the contributions of the talented team at Berrett-Koehler. My special thanks goes to Jeevan Sivasubramaniam, who encouraged me to write about this topic, and Neal Maillet, who supported me so ably throughout the editorial process.

I am also deeply indebted to the hundreds of individuals who contributed their insights and experiences in surveys and interviews. They are too numerous to mention by name, but this is *their* book.

Index

Note: Page numbers in *italics* indicate figures.

About the Author

Bcb Montesdaros

CAROL KINSEY GOMAN, PHD, IS AN international keynote speaker, specializing in leadership and nonverbal communication. She coaches executives, women leaders, salespeople, and managers to build strong and productive business relationships by projecting confidence, credibility, caring, and charisma. A frequent presenter for The Conference Board, The Executive Forum, and the International Association of Business Communicators, Carol presents keynote addresses and seminars on leadership, collaboration, body language in the workplace, and change communication to corporations, government agencies, and major trade associations.

Her clients include more than 100 organizations in 24 countries—corporate giants such as Consolidated Edison, 3M, and PepsiCo; major nonprofit organizations such as the American Institute of Banking, the Healthcare Forum, and the American Society of Training and Development; high-tech firms such as Hewlett-Packard and Texas Instruments; agencies such as the

Office of the Comptroller of the Currency, US Army Tank-Automotive and Armaments Command, and the Library of Congress; and international firms such as Petróleos de Venezuela, Dairy Farm in Hong Kong, SCA Hygiene in Germany, and Wärtsilä Diesel in Finland.

Carol has been cited as an authority in such media as *Industry Week, Investor's Business Daily,* CNN's *Business Unusual,* American Public Media's *Marketplace,* MarketWatch Radio, and *NBC Nightly News.* She is a leadership blogger for Forbes.com and an expert contributor to the *Washington Post*'s "On Leadership" column. She has published more than 300 articles in the fields of organizational change, leadership, innovation, communication, the multigenerational workforce, collaboration, employee engagement, and body language in the workplace. She's the author of 12 business books, including *The Nonverbal Advantage: Secrets and Science of Body Language at Work* and *The Silent Language of Leaders: How Body Language Can Help—or Hurt—How You Lead.*

Carol has served as adjunct faculty at John F. Kennedy University in the international MBA program, at the University of California in the Executive Education Department, and for the Chamber of Commerce of the United States at its Institutes for Organization Management. She's a faculty member for the Institute of Management Studies, presenting training seminars internationally.

To contact Carol about speaking engagements, consulting, or leadership coaching or to register for her newsletter, please e-mail cgoman@ckg.com; call (510) 526-1727; or visit her online at www.ckg.com, www.nonverbaladvantage.com, and www.liarsatwork.com.

Current Speaking Topics

The Silent Language of Leaders:
How Body Language Can Help—or Hurt—How You Lead

Body language is the management of time, space, appearance, posture, gesture, touch, facial expression, eye contact, and voice. When your verbal and nonverbal messages are out of alignment, communication suffers and your messages are weakened. Using body language that supports your business goals is the key to leadership effectiveness—to your ability to project confidence, build relationships of trust, inspire your team, and present content convincingly.

- The two sets of nonverbal signals people look for in leaders—and the circumstances that make one more effective than the other

- Five mistakes your team will make when they read your body language

- How to tell what others really feel about what you just said

  The all-time greatest speaker I have ever worked with. I've worked with Carol numerous times over a 12-year period. She has an incredible rapport and ability to connect with the audience. I've seen her present to an audience of CEOs and totally blow them away. Her material is always original and fresh, and she knows it like a book.

  – Conference Coordinator, The Conference Board

Body Language for Women Leaders:
Traps and Tips for Making an Impact

When first introduced to a leader, people immediately and unconsciously assess her for warmth (empathy, likeability, caring) and authority (power, credibility, status). "Warm" leaders connect with staff in a way that makes people want to do a great job because of that personal connection, affection, and respect. But people also look for leaders who project status and authority, who make them feel secure, and who they believe can follow through and achieve results. Women are champions in the warmth and empathy arena but lose out with power and authority cues—most often because they fall prey to 10 common body language traps.

- Ten body language traps that rob women leaders of their power and authority

- Tips to project instant confidence, credibility, caring, and charisma

- Sharpening your skill at reading body language from head to toes

  Carol spoke at our Global Executive Women's Summit to an appreciative group. Some of their comments: "Really, really informative, applicable, and fun! Thank you." "What a dynamic speaker! And such a useful topic." "She was funny and relevant, and this was an ideal topic for business."

  – Senior Director, Global Learning and Development, Expedia

The Power of Collaborative Leadership: None of Us Is Smarter Than All of Us

Creating collaborative teams that are networked to span organizational boundaries requires a new leadership model—one that replaces command and control with trust and inclusion. The leader's new role is to encourage employees to see themselves as empowered and valued contributors and to help them build their knowledge base, expand their personal networks, and offer their ideas and perspectives in service of a common goal. This program will give you the insight and the skills to build collaborative relationships and to create an environment in which people choose to participate and contribute.

- Why people don't tell what they know— and how to overcome those barriers

- How to build the five levels of trust needed for collaboration

- Body language tips for collaborative leaders

Carol opened our governing board's two-day strategic-planning session with an interactive program on collaboration. Informative and entertaining, her body language tips for collaborative leaders were referred to throughout the rest of the meeting. She was great!

— Executive Director, Northern Rural Training
Employment Consortium

Body Language for Sales and Negotiation: Building Relationships and Closing the Deal

We make major decisions about one another—assessing credibility, trustworthiness, confidence, power, status, and competence—within the first few seconds of meeting. Once someone mentally labels you as "likeable" or "unlikeable," "candid" or "deceptive," everything else you do is viewed through that filter. How convincing you are in sales and negotiation is strongly influenced by unconscious factors such as the way your body postures match the other person, the level of physical activity as you talk, the amount of eye contact you use, and the degree to which you set the tone—literally   of the conversation.

- How to make a positive impression in the first seven seconds—and maintain it throughout the entire meeting

- How to spot the body language signals of uncertainty, resistance, deception, and "ready to buy"

- What to do when faced with nonverbal resistance

  Carol was far and away the best keynote speaker we have ever had at our conventions. She was engaging, interactive, and very practical. Our directors are very excited to begin using her insights right away to improve their sales efforts.

  — President, LearningRx

Communicating Change: Verbal and Nonverbal Messages That Inspire People to Action!

After all the meetings and memos, feedback and focus groups, up to 75 percent of all large-scale change efforts fail. There's a reason why this scenario is so common: *people.* Human beings are complex entities, and all of the strategy sessions in the world won't make a dent in their attitudes and behaviors unless you learn to transform their concerns and fears into confidence and commitment. In most cases, the manner in which change is communicated is more important than the nature of that change.

- ▪ The 10 biggest verbal and nonverbal mistakes leaders make when communicating change

- ▪ The difference between incremental and discontinuous change, and the emotional literacy needed to lead people through both

- ▪ How to help people in your organization (or team or department) go from "surviving change" to "thriving on change"

  Damn! You're good! I spent all day Sunday basking in the reflected glory of your keynote talk opening the night before for our Training Editors Conference. You were witty and inspiring and you suggested remedies that were doable.

  — Program Director, The Freedom Forum Pacific Coast Center

The Truth about Lies in the Workplace: How to Spot Liars, Why We Believe Them, and How to Deal with Them

The Association of Certified Fraud Examiners' business fraud report estimates annual losses in the United States at $3.5 *trillion!* If you knew how to spot deception, you could reduce those costs by hiring the right personnel, choosing the right partners, and believing the right people. When lying in the workplace becomes pervasive, it damages trust, collaboration, and productivity. By creating a high-trust environment, you can decrease destructive lies while liberating employee energy, creativity, and engagement.

- ◼ The five most surprising facts about lies in the workplace

- ◼ Verbal and nonverbal tips for spotting liars at work—
and strategies for dealing with them when you do

- ◼ How to decrease destructive lies by creating
a high-trust work environment

*Carol's high-energy presentation to MBA students at Stanford
was a great hit with our students. I'd strongly encourage others to
work with Carol. She's a pro and a joy!*

**– Director, Mastery in Communication Initiative,
Stanford Graduate School of Business**

Also by Carol Kinsey Goman

The Nonverbal Advantage
Secrets and Science of Body Language at Work

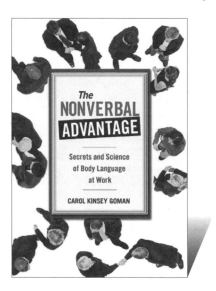

Studies show that we form opinions of one another within seven seconds of meeting and that 60 percent of the messages people receive from us have nothing to do with what we actually say. So the ability to recognize and develop good nonverbal communication skills can be a huge professional advantage.

Carol Kinsey Goman combines the latest research and her years of practical experience in this guide to understanding what you and the people you work with are saying without speaking. Cartoons, photos, entertaining anecdotes, and dozens of simple and enlightening exercises help readers gain control of the messages their bodies are sending so they can project a more accurate and compelling picture of who they really are.

Paperback, 216 pages, ISBN 978-1-57675-492-4
PDF ebook, ISBN 978-1-57675-774-1

BK Berrett–Koehler Publishers, Inc.
San Francisco, *www.bkconnection.com*   800.929.2929

Berrett–Koehler
Publishers

Berrett-Koehler is an independent publisher dedicated to an ambitious mission: *Creating a World That Works for All*.

We believe that to truly create a better world, action is needed at all levels—individual, organizational, and societal. At the individual level, our publications help people align their lives with their values and with their aspirations for a better world. At the organizational level, our publications promote progressive leadership and management practices, socially responsible approaches to business, and humane and effective organizations. At the societal level, our publications advance social and economic justice, shared prosperity, sustainability, and new solutions to national and global issues.

A major theme of our publications is "Opening Up New Space." Berrett-Koehler titles challenge conventional thinking, introduce new ideas, and foster positive change. Their common quest is changing the underlying beliefs, mindsets, institutions, and structures that keep generating the same cycles of problems, no matter who our leaders are or what improvement programs we adopt.

We strive to practice what we preach—to operate our publishing company in line with the ideas in our books. At the core of our approach is stewardship, which we define as a deep sense of responsibility to administer the company for the benefit of all of our "stakeholder" groups: authors, customers, employees, investors, service providers, and the communities and environment around us.

We are grateful to the thousands of readers, authors, and other friends of the company who consider themselves to be part of the "BK Community." We hope that you, too, will join us in our mission.

A BK Life Book

This book is part of our BK Life series. BK Life books change people's lives. They help individuals improve their lives in ways that are beneficial for the families, organizations, communities, nations, and world in which they live and work. To find out more, visit **www.bk-life.com**.

Berrett–Koehler
Publishers

A community dedicated to creating
a world that works for all

Visit Our Website: www.bkconnection.com

Read book excerpts, see author videos and Internet movies, read
our authors' blogs, join discussion groups, download book apps, find
out about the BK Affiliate Network, browse subject-area libraries of
books, get special discounts, and more!

Subscribe to Our Free E-Newsletter, the *BK Communiqué*

Be the first to hear about new publications, special discount offers,
exclusive articles, news about bestsellers, and more! Get on the list
for our free e-newsletter by going to **www.bkconnection.com**.

Get Quantity Discounts

Berrett-Koehler books are available at quantity discounts for orders
of ten or more copies. Please call us toll-free at (800) 929-2929 or
email us at bkp.orders@aidcvt.com.

Join the BK Community

BKcommunity.com is a virtual meeting place where people from
around the world can engage with kindred spirits to create a world
that works for all. BKcommunity.com members may create their own
profiles, blog, start and participate in forums and discussion groups,
post photos and videos, answer surveys, announce and register for
upcoming events, and chat with others online in real time. Please join
the conversation!

Certified

Corporation

bcorporation.net